For a young and c
ence, we are prou
 Situated in the
for mariners from time immemorial — a place to repair and reprovision sailing ships of old and a haven from the tempest, storms, and perils of the deep.

Vincentians are a unique fusion of many cultures — a mix of peoples from many corners of the world, out of which has grown a proud and distinctive identity.

As this fascinating book demonstrates, St Vincent and the Grenadines is rich not only in its wealth of culture and traditions, but also in its natural maritime and agricultural treasures. Together they have helped advance our nation.

The beauty of our islands has also contributed greatly to our progress. Our magnificent palm-shrouded Islands with their silver beaches and sparkling lagoons, have made the islands one of the world's most exclusive and untouched tourist destinations — a paradise for nature lovers, divers, fishermen, watersports enthusiasts, sailors and sun worshippers.

The myriad of marine life is matched only by the spectacular flora, lush tropical vegetation and cascading waterfalls here to be enjoyed by all those who visit. The tiny islands of the Grenadines stand out like pearls on a string in the dazzling waters of the Caribbean Sea where our tradition of hospitality and welcome is without equal.

Thousands of new friends visit us each year to see and enjoy our unique marine heritage: one we are determined to preserve for future generations of Vincentians and for the rest of the world.

Tourism and agriculture are two key areas which have provided an improved quality of life for our citizens. These two sectors contribute the foreign exchange vital to the development of permanent infrastructure for social welfare, health services, and education. In this respect, our achievements in such a short era as an independent nation are cause for pride.

Our ancestors have always welcomed foreigners to our shores, making them guests at their homes. The Vincentians of today, as did their forefathers, maintain this tradition of warmth and friendship. We wish all who visit to share in the joy and glorious beauty of our nation.

Welcome

Andreas Wickam, Director of Tourism

ST VINCENT

CARIBBEAN SUNSEEKERS
St Vincent
& Grenadines

Don Philpott

PASSPORT BOOKS
a division of *NTC Publishing Group*
Lincolnwood, Illinois USA

Published by Passport Books,
a division of NTC Publishing Group,
4255 West Touhy Avenue,
Lincolnwood (Chicago), Illinois
60646 – 1975 USA

ISBN 0 8442 4928 9

© Don Philpott 1996

All rights reserved. No part of this publication may be reproduced, stored in a retrieval system, or transmitted in any form or by any means, electronic, mechanical, photocopying, recording or otherwise without the prior permission of the publishers.

Library of Congress Catalog
Code Numbers: on file

Published by Passport Books in conjunction with
Moorland Publishing Company Ltd.

Color origination by: Reed Reprographics, Ipswich, England
Printed in Hong Kong by Wing King Tong Co Ltd

ACKNOWLEDGMENTS:
Andreas Wickham and Gillian Griffith of the St Vincent and the Grenadines Ministry of Foreign Affairs and Tourism, Dr Earle Kirby, Beachcombers Hotel, Plantation House Hotel, Mustique Company, Cotton House Hotel, Palm Island Beach Club, American Airways and LIAT.

PICTURE CREDITS:
Front cover (large): Walliabou Bay, St Vincent (MPC Picture Collection)
Front Cover (small): Admiralty Bay, Bequia (MPC Picture Collection)
Rear Cover: Jetty near Young Island, St Vincent (MPC Picture Collection)
Title Page: Friendship Bay, Bequia (MPC Picture Collection)
The Cotton House (Cheryl Andrews Marketing): pp98, 99; Palm Island: p102; Don Philpott: pp43, 46, 51, 74, 75, 79, 82, 110. The other illusrations are from the MPC Picture Collection.

MPC Production Team:
Editorial & Design: John Robey; *Cartography:* Mark Titterton

DISCLAIMER

While every care has been taken to ensure that the information in this book is as accurate as possible at the time of publication, the publishers and author accept no responsibility for any loss, injury or inconvenience sustained by anyone using this book.

Your trip to the Caribbean should be a happy one, but certain activities such as water sports should be approached with care and under proper supervision when appropriate. It is also in your own interests to check locally about flora and fauna that it is best to avoid.

Contents

Foreword 1

Before You Go 7
- Getting to St Vincent & the Grenadines 8
- Location & the Landscape 9
- History 12
- Climate 21
- The People 21
- Culture 23
- The Economy 24
- The Government & Judiciary 24
- Plant & Animal Life 25
- The Islands' Fruits 32
- Food 41
- Drink 45

Touring & Exploring St Vincent
- Getting Around St Vincent 47
- St Vincent 52
- Kingstown 52
- Other Places to Visit 57
- The West Coast 64
- The South Coast 72
- Mesopotamia & the East Coast 73

Touring & Exploring The Grenadines
- Bequia 87
- Canouan 96
- Mustique 97
- Mayreau 100
- Tobago Cays 101
- Palm Island 101
- Petit St Vincent 101
- Union Island 102

Traveller's Tips 110

Eating Out
- In & Around Kingstown 83
- On the West Coast 84
- In the South 84
- On the East Coast 85
- On the Grenadines
  - Bequia 105
  - Canouan 108
  - Mustique 108
  - Mayreau 108
- Union Island 109

Index 142

KEY TO SYMBOLS USED IN TEXT MARGIN AND ON MAPS

- 🚶 Recommended walks
- 🏛 Museum
- ✱ Other place of interest
- 🏖 Beach
- 🏰 Fort
- ❁ Garden
- ⛪ Church/Ecclesiastical site
- ⌘ Building of interest
- ☀ Beautiful view/Scenery, Natural phenomenon
- 🐦 Birdlife
- ⛩ Archaeological Site

KEY TO MAPS

- ——— Main Routes (Surfaced)
- – – – Path
- ▪▪▪▪▪ Tunnel
- ▬ Town
- ○ Village
- ～ River

HOW TO USE THIS GUIDE

Enjoying as much sun and fun on a vacation is everyone's dream. Caribbean Sunseekers: *St Vincent & Grenadines* will help to make this dream come true.

Your guide has been designed in three easy to use sections.

'Before You Go' is packed with detailed information on the island, its history, geography, people, culture, food and much more. 'Touring and Exploring St Vincent' is a comprehensive itinerary covering the island with a series of useful and practical motoring or walking tours. Many places are off the beaten track and not on the usual tourist circuit.

'Traveller's Tips' arranged in alphabetical order for easy reference, lists practical information and useful advice to help you plan your vacation before you go and while you are there.

Distinctive margin symbols in the text and on maps, plus places to visit highlighted in bold enable the reader to find the most interesting places with ease.

Before You Go

St Vincent and the necklace of islands that make up the Grenadines are some of the most unspoiled islands in the Caribbean with spectacular landscapes, stunning beaches of golden sand, and crystal clear turquoise waters which attract divers and sailors from around the world. The Grenadines, in particular, boast some of the most exclusive holiday islands in the world and have long attracted the very rich and the famous.

St Vincent and the Grenadines are in no way typical tourist islands, and nor do they need to be. Their great attraction is their natural beauty, the warmth and friendliness of the people who live here, and the near year-round sunshine.

Wallilabou Bay — one of the numerous secluded coves on St Vincent

Life on St Vincent and the Grenadines is easy going and it is the ideal place to unwind and relax and soak up the sun. The food is fresh and good, the sea is warm and the hospitality generous.

You can watch or join in an impromptu game of cricket on the beach, head off to explore delightful secluded coves, go walking, cycling or snorkelling, take a trip to some of the surrounding islands, or just wander around this delightful, friendly island discovering its fascinating charm, customs and traditions.

GETTING TO ST VINCENT & THE GRENADINES

By Air

The main airport is on St Vincent but there are also small airports on Bequia, Canouan, Mustique and Union Island.

While there are no direct international flights to St Vincent and the Grenadines, there are same day connections with LIAT from the main gateways of Barbados, Grenada, Martinique, St Lucia, San Juan and Trinidad. International airlines serving these gateways include Air Canada, Air France, American Airlines, BWIA and British Airways.

LIAT has scheduled flights from St Vincent to Anguilla, Antigua, Barbados, Caracas, Carriacou, Grenada, Guadeloupe, Georgetown-Guyana, Montserrat, Nevis, Port of Spain, San Juan, St Croix, St Lucia, St Maarten, St Thomas and Union Island. Several of these flights involve one or more stops en route. From Union Island LIAT have scheduled services to Caracas, Carriacou, Grenada, Guadeloupe, Martinique, Port of Spain, St Lucia and St Vincent.

Carib Express, which was launched in 1995, is based in Barbados, and operates the only jet service between the islands, flying 146s which require relatively short runways for take-off and landing. It flies between Barbados, Grenada, Dominica (Melville Hall), St Lucia (Vigie), St Vinent, as well as Tobago and Port of Spain.

Air Martinique also flies scheduled services to Mustique and Union Island and several Caribbean destinations, while Mustique Airways flies between Barbados, Mustique and St Vincent. Mustique Airways and St Vincent and Grenadine Air (SVG Air), also have planes that can be chartered for private travel, sightseeing and photography.

The St Vincent and Grenadines Tourist Board has an information desk in the arrival hall of the Grantley Adams International Airport in Barbados, which is manned daily between 1pm and 8pm to assist visitors travelling on to the islands.

By Boat

Cruise ships dock at Kingstown in St Vincent and often visit the other Grenadines. Cruise lines visiting the islands include Chandris, Epirotiki, Ocean Line Cruises, Pacquet Cruises, Princess Cruises, Sun Line, Windjammer and Windstar.

There are regular ferry services between St Vincent and the Grenadines as far south as Union Island. For visiting yachts there are ports of entry at Kingstown and Wallilabou Bay on St Vincent, and entry formalities and registration can also be undertaken on Bequia, Mustique, Union Island, Canouan, Ottley Hall and Campden Park.

LOCATION & THE LANDSCAPE

St Vincent and the Grenadines is in the Windward Islands and part of the Lesser Antilles in the eastern Caribbean. St Vincent is about 21 miles (34km) southwest of St Lucia, and 100 miles (160km) west of Barbados. It is to the north of the Grenadines, and altogether, there are thirty-two islands spread out in a 60 mile (100km) long arc reaching down to Petit St Vincent just a stone's throw from Petit Martinique, which is part of Grenada.

By a quirk of the Treaty of Versailles, a line was drawn through the Grenadines putting them under the jurisdiction of either St Vincent or Grenada. For some reason, the architects of this plan insisted on drawing a straight line which actually passes through the northernmost tip of both Carriacou and Petit Martinique.

Saint Vincent is 18 miles (28km) long and at its widest, 11 miles (17km) across. It covers an area of 133 sq miles (347 sq km) Bequia lies 9 miles (14km) south of St Vincent and is the largest of the Grenadines with an area of about 7 sq miles (18 sq km). The other main islands are Union Island which covers 3.2 sq miles (8.3 sq km), Canouan with an area of 3 sq miles (7.8 sq km), Mustique covering 2 sq miles (5.2 sq km), Mayreau 1 sq mile (2.6 sq km), Palm Island and Petit St Vincent both about 110 acres. There are many other tiny uninhabited islands including the stunning Tobago Cays.

Altogether the territory of St Vincent and the Grenadines

SUNSEEKER HOT SPOTS

BEQUIA
scenery, boat trips, walking, historic sites, diving, beaches
page 87-96

KINGSTOWN
market, churches, historic buildings, shopping
page 52

KINGSTOWN BOTANICAL GARDENS & MUSEUM
scenery, natural history, walks
page 58-9, 60-1

ISLAND CRUISES
Mustique, Palm Island, Union Island
page 48-9

LAYOU
beaches, walks, wildlife, historic sites, petroglyphs
page 65-8

**MESOPOTAMIA
(MARRIAQUA VALLEY)**
scenery, walks, historic sites, wildlife
page 73-6

SOUFRIERE
volcanic area, scenery, wildlife, hiking
page 78

VERMONT NATURE TRAILS
wildlife, walks, scenery
page 65

YOUNG ISLAND & FORT DUVERNETTE
beaches, diving, watersports, historic site
page 72

— BEFORE YOU GO —

BEACHES

St Vincent and the islands of the Grenadines have fabulous beaches, everything you ever dreamed of for a tropical island, with sands ranging in colour from glorious golden to jet black, fringed with tall palms for shade, and turquoise clear warm seas. Generally the best swimming beaches are on the protected western coasts. There are many lovely black sand beaches on the windier Atlantic Ocean coast but these tend to have choppier seas. For the experienced they offer excellent surfing and windsurfing, but swimming is not advised. Always check locally for any swimming risks.

The Top Beaches

St Vincent: Blue Lagoon, Indian Bay, Villa Beach, Peter's Hope, Kearton Bay, Buccament Bay, Richmond Beach

Bequia: Lower Bay, Princess Margaret Beach, Friendship Bay, Spring Bay, Admiralty Bay

Mustique: Endeavour Bay, L'Ansecoy, Macaroni, Gelliceaux

Canouan: All the beaches

Mayreau: Salt Whistle, Saline Bay

Union Island: Chatham Bay, Big Sand Beach

Palm Island: Casuarina Beach

Tanning Safely

The sun is very strong but sea breezes often disguise just how hot it is. If you are not used to the sun, take it carefully for the first two or three days, use a good sun screen with a factor of 15 or higher, and do not sunbathe during the hottest parts of the day. Wear sunglasses and a sun hat. Sunglasses will protect you against the glare, especially strong on the beach, and sun hats will protect your head.

If you spend a lot of time swimming or scuba diving, take extra care, as you will burn even quicker because of the combination of salt water and sun.

Calamine lotion and preparations containing aloe are both useful in combating sunburn.

covers almost 150 sq miles (388 sq km).

St Vincent is a lush volcanic island with mountains running north to south down the centre of the island. These mountains have steep, densely wooded slopes with many fast moving streams flowing down them. Few of the streams are very large or long, and water flow is heaviest after rain. There are no navigable rivers on the island.

The volcano Soufrière in the north of the island is the highest peak at 4,048ft (1,234m). The volcano is still active and last erupted in 1979 causing widespread evacuation and considerable damage to surrounding agricultural land and crops. This eruption was not as severe as the two major eruptions in 1812 and 1902. In 1902 Soufrière erupted at the same time as Mount Pelée on Martinique. The devastation was awesome and the entire northern half of St Vincent was devastated. These eruptions have, however, deposited a layer of rich fertile ash which have produced the lush vegetation that covers most of the island, particularly in the Mesopotamia Valley. The eastern coast has cliffs and largely rocky beaches with choppy seas and surf because of the onshore winds, while the western, sheltered coastline has fine beaches and safe swimming.

Most of the larger Grenadine islands have hills, and some of the smaller ones are little more than islets.

HISTORY

St Vincent is believed to have been named by Christopher Columbus because he first sighted the island on January 22, 1498 — St Vincent's Day.

Long before he 'discovered' the island, however, it had been settled by the peaceful Ciboney who had paddled their way north in their dug-out canoes from their original homelands in South America. The Ciboney, part of the Arawak Amerindian race, are believed to have first landed on St Vincent around 5000BC and there was a sizeable population about the end of the first century AD.

Their peace was shattered by the warlike Caribs, also from South America, who had a fearsome reputation. They arrived about 1000AD, and by the time the first Europeans arrived, the Caribs dominated the islands. It was reported that the Caribs were cannibals and feasted on the bodies of prisoners, and while there is no evidence to support this, it might explain why Europeans gave the island a wide berth for much of the next 200 years. There was also little need to colonise the island at first because the French and British were more interested in fighting over St Lucia just to the north.

The French tried to establish a settlement in 1626, but they were ousted by the English the following year, after the island had been granted to the Earl of Carlisle by Charles I.

In the following years there were many attempts to settle the island by the Dutch, English and French but most failed because of Carib hostility.

Among the first successful settlers from across the Atlantic were Africans, slaves who were shipwrecked off Bequia in 1675. They managed to swim ashore in the Grenadines and many then made their way through the islands to St Vincent where they settled, with many marrying the native Caribs. The descendants of these Black-Caribs, as they were known, still live on St Vincent.

The French had again established a small settlement on St Vincent in the 1720s at the request of the native Caribs who thought that the Black Caribs were becoming too dominant. The French introduced the first African slaves to work their plantations. The Black Caribs, to avoid capture and a return to slavery, moved into the hills. They fiercely resisted attempts to dislodge them, and tales of their opposition spread through the islands, encouraging many slaves to escape and try to join them. While some did make it to St Vincent, most perished trying to cross the dangerous seas in makeshift boats and rafts.

In 1748 the Treaty of Aix-la-Chapelle was signed between the British and French and this was intended to bring peace to the eastern Caribbean. Rather than fight over the islands, it was agreed that St Lucia, St Vincent and Dominica be declared neutral territory. The peace, however, was short lived and the island changed hands several times as the two nations fought over possession.

In 1762, during the Seven Years' War, the British General Robert Monckton captured St Vincent and the Treaty of Paris in 1763, ceded it to Britain.

The British immediately set about settling the island, despite opposition from the Caribs who refused to accept their rule. The next few decades were a turbulent time in St Vincent's history with constant battles between the

AN INTERESTING HISTORICAL THEORY

Eminent island historian Dr Earle Kirby, who is also curator of the Kingstown museum, believes there is some evidence that Africans actually made their own way to St Vincent long before the first Europeans arrived. And, he suggests, this better explains why these European settlers found Black Caribs already living there, rather than stories about escaped slaves and others being shipwrecked.

According to Dr Kirby, the presence of Black Caribs was mentioned quite early in the colonists tenure of the area, so how is it that there were enough slaves to run away from the sugar plantations which were yet to be established?

The penalty exacted from a runaway slave was usually death by being thrown into a *tayche* (copper) of boiling syrup, often after being tortured. This was considered an adequate deterrent to escape, and Dr Kirby thinks it unlikely that sufficient slaves managed to escape and remain at large to provide the numbers of negroid people needed to populate the villages that were found.

He quotes a legend in Martinique and Guadeloupe of estate owners introducing the poisonous fer-de-lance snakes as a further deterrent to escape. The snakes were placed in deep trenches around the plantation and slave's sleeping quarters, but contrary to popular belief, these snakes were actually endemic to the islands, so stories of their introduction are false.

The Black Caribs in St Vincent had a well organised society and must have been here for years before any addition to their numbers could have resulted from escaped slaves. And, after they were deported to Roatan in the Gulf of Honduras in 1797, some migrated to Honduras where they joined with other negroid people who called themselves the Garifuna. This name was also adopted by those from Roatan who migrated to Southern Belize in the early 1800s.

In Guatemala there is a legend that the negroes in the coast adjacent to Belize, arrived there in a large group led by a white man.

Dr Kirby argues that this white man was not white in complexion, but white from being covered by long flowing white robes, and his head being covered by a white turban, like Abubakari II of Mali, or one of his senior officers in the thirteenth century. And, there are a number of facts which would seem to support this.

Writer Ivan van Sertima, in his book *They came before Columbus*, devotes a chapter to Abubakari II, 'The Mariner Prince of Mali', which ends with the words: 'Then one day, dressed in a flowing white robe, and a jewelled turban, he took leave of Mali and set out with his fleet down the Senegal, heading west across the Atantic, never to return. He took his Griot and half his history with him.'

During his researches, Dr Kirby has also come across two other pieces of circumstantial evidence which add weight to his theory.

In two small islands in the Grenadines — Union Island and Carriacou — there is a ceremony called 'The Big Drum Dance' which is performed towards the end of the dry season and its incantations are hoped to make the rain fall. This ritual must have come as a whole from a group of people who had performed it in Africa. With the precautions taken on slave ships to prevent friends or family being aboard the same slave ship, it is very unlikely for a ceremony to have been introduced from a group which had been transported on a slave ship.

There is also a mention of 'Garifuna' in Thurn's book *Among the Indians of Guiana*. The word means 'people of the savannahs', and Dr Kirby argues that the use of this same word to refer to the negroid people in Honduras, Guatemala and Belize, rules out the mountainous island of St Vincent, and must go back way beyond 1797. It is much more likely that it refers to Mali which is certainly savannah country, on the edge of the Sahara desert.

This also ties in with the Big Drum Dance as having its origins in a savannah area. On another small island in the Grenadines — Canouan — was found an adorno from a pottery vessel of an effigy of an African head with what appears to be Yoruba tribal marks on its cheeks, this was made in the style of the Caribs — who were the dominant people in the southern islands of the Eastern Caribbean — from about 1200AD until the Europeans ousted them in 1772 in St Vincent and exiled them in 1797.

Additional circumstantial evidence is found in a shallow rock shelter at Buccament on the calm leeward side of St Vincent, about 200yd from the sea. At the back of the shelter there are several lines of script many metres long. Many pieces of Arabic script have been identified, and meanings have been supplied for some groups of letters, among them being 'Mohammed', and the characters for 'Allah' were recognised.

Dr Kirby concludes that the progenitors of the Black Caribs (later called Garifuna) were not the unwilling passengers in the holds of slave ships, but could very well be willing crews on the several ships of Abubakari's fleet of exploration which sailed out of history from West Africa, across 'the wine dark sea', to re-appear as patchwork villages on the quilt along the shores of the Caribbean.

British and the Caribs, who conducted a highly successful guerilla war. This was the period of the First Carib Wars.

In 1779 the French who were supporting the American colonies in their War of Independence, attacked St Vincent and overran the island with hardly a shot being fired.

The French force landed in three warships, and their intelligence was obviously good, because all the soldiers from the garrison which should have been protecting Kingstown had been transported to the north of the island to help gather the harvest on the Governor's plantation. It is also reported that the officer in charge of the soldiers took with him the keys to the gun battery, so that even if someone had wanted to man the guns, they could not have gained access to them.

The French remained in control until the Treaty of Versailles in 1783 which restored the island to Britain again. Over the next few years, confrontations between the British and Caribs increased, leading to the Carib uprising in 1795, the Second Carib War.

The French Revolution had brought turmoil to the French-speaking West Indies, and all slaves working on estates on the islands had been given their freedom — albeit temporarily as slavery was re-introduced when it was realised there was no one to work the estates for the pittance the owners were prepared to pay.

French militants from Martinique and Guadeloupe, and their newly freed slaves, backed the Caribs in their rebellion. The Caribs attacked the plantations, and it is said that many estate owners met horrible deaths being crushed to death in their own sugar cane presses.

The Caribs conducted a fierce campaign. Their numbers were split into two forces, one led by Duvallé which quickly stormed down the east coast destroying all the plantations it overran, and the other, led by Carib chieftain Chatoyer, which fought its way down the west coast but sparing most of the plantations. The two armies met in the south and under the command of Chatoyer, took up positions on the hills overlooking Kingstown where the retreating British troops had taken shelter. The whole island, apart from Kingstown, had fallen to the Caribs.

The local militia backed by a strong force of British troops, however, crept out of Kingstown at night and made a surprise dawn attacked on the Carib positions on Dorsetshire Hill. The attack was led by Major Alexander Leith who is said to have killed Chatoyer in hand-to-hand combat. Chatoyer was said to have been wearing a silver gorget, a piece of throat armour, personally presented to him by Prince William, later King William 1V, during his visit to the island.

With their chieftain slain, many of the Black Caribs retreated again to the densely wooded interior. Fighting continued for several months but resistance was slowly and harshly crushed. Many of their settlements had been stormed and razed to the ground, and their fields and crops were destroyed. In 1796 General Abercromby delivered an ultimatum to the Caribs which was surrender or be wiped out.

Almost 5,000 Caribs gave themselves up, and nearly all of these were deported to Roatan, one of the Bay Islands off Honduras and Belize, where there is still a large community today.

Major Leith earned promotion to Colonel and a plaque in his honour was placed in the Anglican Cathedral, while after Independence, Chatoyer was declared a National Hero.

With Emancipation in 1834 all slaves in the British colonies were freed, although they all had to serve an 'apprenticeship' in which they agreed to continue to work free of charge for their old owners for a further four years. Once this apprenticeship was over, most of the freed slaves started to farm for themselves on small plots that they cleared from the forest.

This led to a shortage of labour to work on the estates, largely producing sugar cane, Sea Island cotton and arrowroot, and so Portuguese and East Indian labourers were imported as indentured workers in the second half of the nineteenth century. Again, many of these indentured workers agreed to work for free in return for board and lodging, and the promise of a grant of land at the end of their commitment.

A census conducted in 1891 found that of the 41,054 population, 'just over 3,000 were whites and Hindu coolies, the rest being Negroes and people of mixed blood'. Kingstown had a population of 6,000.

As sugar beet was planted widely throughout northern Europe in the late nineteenth century, the price of sugar cane crashed, and St Vincent suffered a long depression, not helped by the hurricane which hit the island in 1898 and the volcanic eruption in 1902 which wiped out almost all agricultural production in the

SHOPPING

Shops are usually open between 8am and noon and 1pm to 4pm Monday to Friday, and between 8am to around noon on Saturday. There is an increasing trend for larger stores not to close over lunch, and to remain open later in the evening.

There is a good range of souvenirs and gifts, including locally made handicrafts, batik wear and goods, leather goods, wood carvings and paintings by island artists. Many of the T-shirts sold are hand painted, so do not be too dismissive. There are also several shops selling duty-free goods such as jewellery, watches, perfumes, crystal glass, figurines and china. Noah's Arkade on Bay Street, Kingstown, has gifts and several books about the island and its history, culture and folklore. The market is also a good source of interesting gifts, especially spices and products such as jams, jellies and syrups made from them.

Ancient artifacts in the museum in the Botanical Gardens, Kingstown

BEFORE YOU GO

An ancient stone axehead, recovered from an archaeolgical site on St Vincent. Many such artifacts from the original inhabitants of the islands may be seen in the museum at the Botanical Gardens

These cannons at Admiralty Bay, Bequia, are a reminder of the area's colonial past

north of the island, and claimed more than 2,000 lives. Agricultural exports which were worth £166,753 in 1883 had fallen in value to £81,837 in 1888.

Economic recovery was slow although St Vincent became a leading exporter of bananas and arrowroot, the mainstay of its twentieth-century agriculture.

In 1958 St Vincent became a member of the West Indies Federation, it received its new constitution in 1960, and became a State in Association with Britain, responsible for its own internal affairs, on October 27, 1969. St Vincent has been a member of the Caribbean Free Trade Area since July 1968.

In 1972 plans were put forward for a Federated State of St Vincent, St Lucia and Grenada, but these failed to materialise, and on 27 October 1979, St Lucia and the Grenadines gained full independence.

The Government was established as a constitutional monarchy and became a member of the Commonwealth. The first post-independence elections were won by the Labour Party in December 1979, and Milton Cato became the first Prime Minister.

On 8 December 1979, the Government had to quell a brief uprising on Union Island, attributed to economic problems following the eruption of Soufrière in April. The eruption lasted for ten days, damaging agriculture and the new tourist industry, and caused widespread evacuation although there was no loss of life, and in 1980 Hurricane Allen struck the island, devastating the banana crop.

The Prime Minister adopted a centralist line, critical of the revolution in Grenada and developments in Jamaica and Guyana, while seeking closer ties with Barbados, and Trinidad and Tobago.

In July 1984 the New Democratic Party won the general election, and leader Bequian James Fitz-Allen Mitchell immediately embarked on an ambitious programme to boost employment, re-organise agriculture and encourage tourism. This policy was largely successful and heralded a building boom on the island, although high unemployment continued to be a major problem. In May 1989 James Mitchell was re-elected to his second five-year term with his party winning all fifteen parliamentary seats.

In July 1989 fire broke out in the police barracks in Kingstown, and quickly spread destroying a large part of the centre of town. The ensuing rebuilding programme was also geared at boosting tourism, and this increased to such an extent that in 1990, the number of cruise ships visiting the island had to be restricted to prevent overcrowding. In 1991 the banana industry, which accounted for almost half the country's export earnings, started a three-year replanting programme, although its future is uncertain largely because of political decisions being taken in Brussels and elsewhere, and outside its control. The Prime Minister was elected to his third term of office in 1994.

CLIMATE

The island enjoys a tropical maritime climate and stands in the path of the north-west trade winds. Summer temperatures average around 90°F (32°C) in Kingstown, and rarely drop below 64°F (18°C). It is usually a degree or two cooler on the east coast because of the prevailing winds.

Annual rainfall varies from around 60in (150cm) around the coast to 150in (375cm) in the mountains. The dry season is from January to late April/early May with the rains starting in late June/early July and continuing on and off for the rest of the year, with the heaviest rainfalls between July and October. St Vincent and the Grenadines lie in the hurricane belt and although these do not come ashore very often, when they do hit it can be devastating. Major hurricanes have hit the island in 1780, 1898 and more recently, in 1980.

THE PEOPLE

St Vincent and the Grenadines has a population of about 107,000, and almost 99,000 live on St Vincent. Bequia's population is around 4,850, and Union Island about 1,900. Almost three-quarters of the population are of African origin, and another fifth are of mixed descent, there is a small minority of European descendants and a smaller group of East Indian descent. While there are few descendants of the originally Carib settlers, there is a small group of Black Caribs, of African-Amerindian descent, and a group which has figured prominently in the island's history.

The main language is English although a patois is widely spoken, but it is almost impossible for visitors to understand this. Almost half the population are Anglican and the other main religions are

Passengers waiting at Port Elizabeth, Bequia for the ferry from St Vincent

— BEFORE YOU GO —

Kingstown market is a good place to see local life

Roman Catholic and Methodist. Primary school education is free but not compulsory, and most secondary school education is provided by bodies with religious affiliations.

St Vincent is divided into five parishes — St George in the south which includes Kingstown, Charlotte which takes in most of the eastern side of the island, St Andrew which runs between Kingstown and Layou, St Patrick which runs between Layou and just south of Troumaca, and St David which covers the remaining north western part of the island.

CULTURE

One of the great attractions of St Vincent and the Grenadines is its mix of culture. It is a blend of centuries of English tradition, African heritage and more than a trace of French, all shaken together with West Indian and Creole customs, habits and lifestyles. This is reflected in island dance, music and folk music, costume and even cooking. And, Carnival, or Vincy Mas, is the time for all these ingredients to be put together for the celebration to end all celebrations.

The island boasts many talented artists and sculptors, wood carvers and potters. The St Vincent Craftsmen's Centre on the outskirts of Kingstown, illustrates the wide range of arts and crafts practised, from hand silk-screened clothing and wall hangings, to island jewellery, and from perfect replica model boats to paintings of island scenes, which provide a permanent memento of your stay on the island. Bequia is noted for its model-boat makers, and up and coming artist Silvanus Simmons, who although only 19, is already an accomplished artist and modeller. Some of his murals of Bequia landscapes can be admired on the walls of the harpoon Saloon in Port Elizabeth, and elsewhere.

THE ECONOMY

Agriculture, fishing and to a less extent, forestry, have always been and still are the backbone of the island's economy, although tourism is of increasing economic importance. Major crops grown include banana, the leading export, and arrowroot, of which St Vincent is one of the world's major producers. It is used in cooking for thickening sauces, and is widely used in biscuit making and the manufacture of some paper, especially computer printout stationery. Other crops produced include nutmeg, ginger, yams, sweet potatoes, root crops, plantains and carrots. Plantains and carrots are exported to neighbouring islands, and a lot of fruit and vegetables are sent to Barbados, which although it is heavily agricultural, is largely planted with sugar cane. Forest covers almost half the island, and wood is used for charcoal burning, and there is inshore and offshore fishing.

Most industry is based on processing agricultural crops, including the production of soap and edible oils from coconuts. There are also rum distilleries, copra processing plants and flour mills. Other industries include boat building and a plant which produces boxes in which bananas are packed for export.

THE GOVERNMENT & JUDICIARY

St Vincent and the Grenadines is

an independent republic within the Commonwealth. The British Queen is head of state and is represented on the island by the Governor-General. There is a single legislative chamber, the House of Assembly, consisting of both elected representatives and senators appointed by the Governor-General. The Prime Minister is the leader of the majority party, and leads the Government.

St Vincent is a member of the East Caribbean Supreme Court with a high court and appeals court, with recourse to the Privy Council as the final court of appeal.

PLANT & ANIMAL LIFE

The lush vegetation and animal life are part of the island's great charm, and there can be few more lush panoramas than the one that greets you as you look down over the fertile Mesopotamia Valley, a few miles north-east of Kingstown. From your vantage point overlooking the valley, you can see thousands of acres of fertile fields producing many of the fruit and vegetable crops that find their way to Kingstown market. There are palms of all descriptions, giant ferns and bamboos, bananas, coconut groves, hanging breadfruit, mango, nutmeg, cocoa and pawpaw, and the most stunning array of spectacularly coloured flowering plants from giant African tulip trees festooned with scarlet blossom to tiny orchids. Bougainvillea flowers everywhere, there are scores of varieties of hibiscus, frangipani and poinsettia. There are heliconia, also known as the lobster plant, bird of paradise flowers and anthurium everywhere. The flamboyant tree is also known as the tourist tree because it bursts into bloom during the summer and is a blaze of colour.

Around Soufrière, because of the frequent eruptions and altitude, there is typical elfin woodland.

Along the coast there are swamps, mangroves and marsh woodlands, while inland there are breathtaking walks through tropical rain forests.

Beach morning glory with its array of pink flowers is found on many beaches, and is important because its roots help prevent sand drift. The plant also produces nectar from glands in the base of its leaf stalks which attract ants, and it is thought this evolution has occurred so that the ants will discourage any

Flowers bloom all year round throughout the islands

Bougainvillaea — with its bracts of a range of different hues — grows almost everywhere on St Vincent and the Grenadines

leaf-nibbling predators. Other beach plants include seagrape and the manchineel, which should be treated with caution.

Of course, the sea teems with brilliantly coloured fish and often, even more spectacularly coloured coral and marine plants. Even if you just float upside down in the water with a face mask on, you will be able to enjoy many of the beautiful underwater scenes, but the best way to see things is by scuba diving, snorkelling or taking a trip in one of the many glass bottomed boats. Sports fish include barracuda, kingfish, Spanish mackerel, blue runner, sailfish, marlin, tuna and bonito.

There are scores of different multi-coloured corals that make up the reefs offshore. There are hard and soft corals and only one — the fire coral poses a threat to swimmers and divers, because if touched, it causes a stinging skin rash.

Among the more spectacular corals are deadman's fingers, staghorn, brain coral and seafans, and there are huge sea anemones and sponges, while tropical fish species include the parrotfish, blue tang surgeonfish, tiny but aggressive damselfish, angelfish and brightly coloured wrasse.

Coastal swamps also provide a rich habitat for wildlife. Tiny tree crabs and burrowing edible land crabs scurry around in the mud trapped in the roots of mangrove trees just above water level. Herons, egrets, pelicans and often frigate birds roost in the higher branches, the mangrove cuckoo shares the lower branches with belted kingfishers.

Inland, gardens are generally a blaze of colour with flowers in bloom year round, growing alongside exotic vegetables like yam, sweet potato, and dasheen. Flowering plants include the flamboyant tree with its brilliant red flowers which burst into bloom in early summer, and long dark brown seed pods, up to 2ft (0.6m) long which can be used as rattles when the seeds have dried out inside.

Bougainvillaea grows everywhere and seems to be in bloom year round in a host of different colours, In fact, the colour does not come from petals but the plants bract-like leaves which surround the small petal-less flowers.

There are yellow and purple allamandas, poinsettia, hibiscus, anthurium and multi-coloured flowers of the ixora.

The leaves of the traveller's palm spread out like a giant open fan, and the tree got its name because the fan was believed to point from south to north, but it rarely does.

The flowers attract hummingbirds like the doctorbird, as well as the carib grackle, a strutting, starling-like bird with a paddle-shaped tail, and the friendly bananaquit. You can also spot tree lizards, and the larger geckos which hunt at night.

Along roadsides and hedgerows in the countryside, you can see the vinelike caralita, calabash with its gourd-like fruits, tamarind and distinctive star-shaped leaves of the castor bean, whose seeds when crushed yield castor oil.

The areas of scrubland have their own flora or fauna, with plants bursting into colour following the first heavy rains after the dry season. There are century plants, with their prickly, sword - like leaves, which grow for up to twenty years before flowering. The yellow flower stalk grows at a tremendous rate for several days and can reach 20ft (6m) tall, but having bloomed once the whole plant then dies.

Other typical scrubland vegetation includes aloe, acacia, prickly pear and several species of cactus. Fiddlewood provides hard timber for furniture, highly coloured variegated crotons, the white flowered, aromatic frangipani and sea island cotton, which used to provide the very finest cotton. Scrub vegetation also plays host to birds such as the mockingbird, ground dove, kingbird and grassquit, and it is the ideal habitat for lizards.

The rainforests provide the most prolific vegetation with giant gommier and mahogany trees with their fascinating black and red seeds, much used for necklaces. There are magnificent swathes of giant ferns, towering bamboo groves, enormous air plants, and a host of flowering or variegated plants such as heliconia, philodendron and wild fuchsia. There are balsa wood trees, the world's lightest wood, the flowering vine marcgravia, and the prolific mountain cabbage palm, and among the foliage and flowers you can find hummingbirds and parrots.

The animal life on the island is not diverse and there are few large animals. There are frogs and toads which croak loudly all night, lizards and snakes such as the poisonous fer-de-lance, allegedly introduced by the plantation owners and kept in perimeter ditches round the estate to deter slaves from escaping. Mongooses, which grow up to 2ft (0.6m) in length including tail, were said to have been introduced to the islands to kill rats gnawing at the

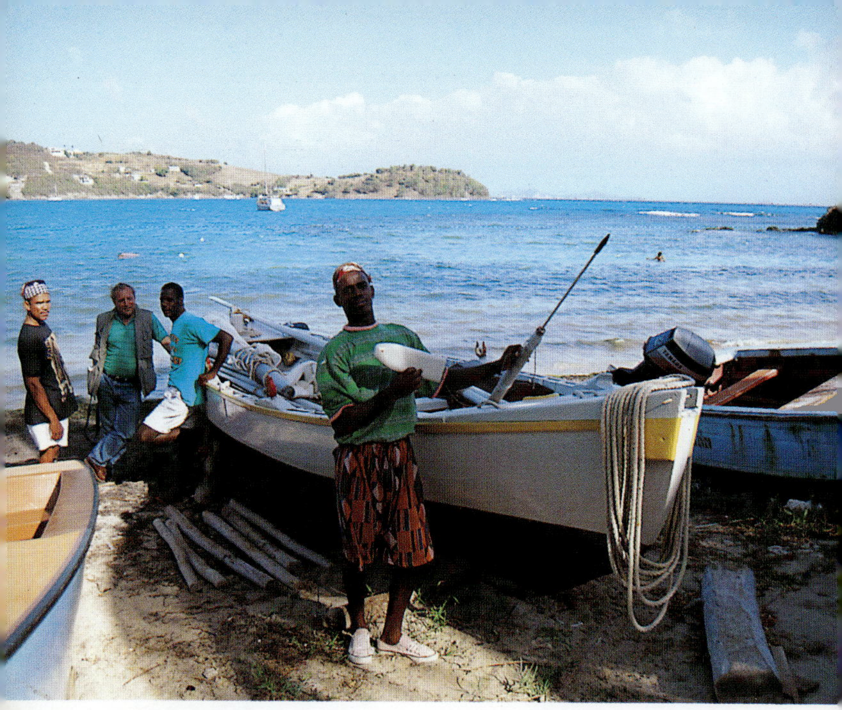

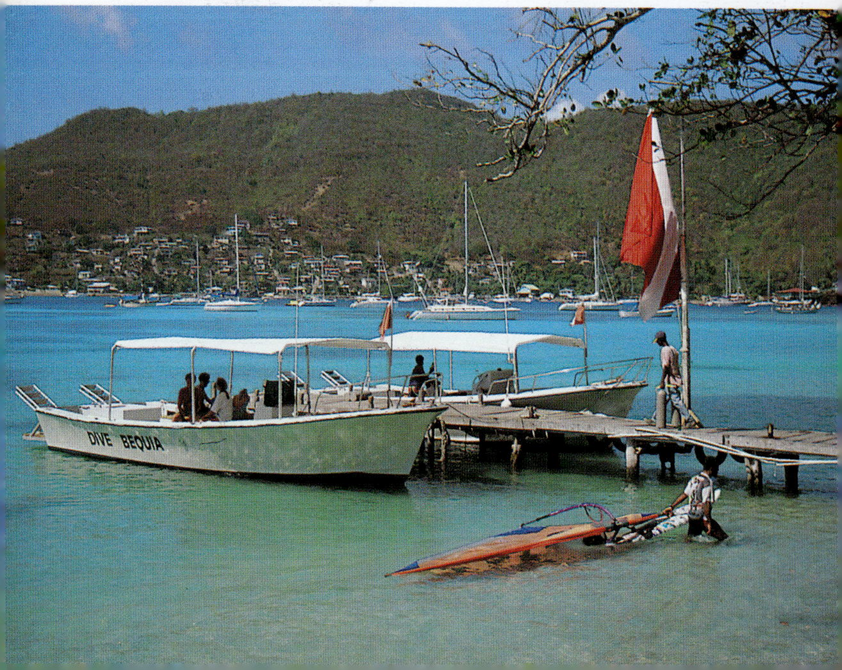
DIVE BEQUIA

THE MANCHINEEL TREE — A NOTE OF WARNING

The manchineel, which can be found on many beaches, has a number of effective defensive mechanisms which can prove very painful. Trees vary from a few feet to more than 30 feet in height, and have widely spreading, deep forked boughs with small, dark green leaves and yellow stems, and fruit like small, green apples. If you examine the leaves carefully without touching them, you will notice a small pin-head sized raised dot at the junction of leaf and leaf stalk. The apple-like fruit is poisonous, and sap from the tree causes very painful blisters. It is so toxic, that early Caribs are said to have dipped their arrow heads in it before hunting trips. Sap is released if a leaf or branch is broken, and more so after rain. Avoid contact with the tree, do not sit under it, or on a fallen branch, and do not eat the fruit. If you do get sap on your skin, run into the sea and wash it off as quickly as possible.

---

sugar cane. There is also a story that they were introduced to kill the fer-de-lance.

There are also the shy agouti and shuffling armadillo.

Another unusual animal is the manicou, a small opossum, and introduced to the island from Dominica at the beginning of the twentieth century. It lives in trees and forages over huge areas at night, and is not averse to rooting through trash cans for any delicacies.

Lumbering sea turtles also come ashore at night between March and August to lay their eggs in the sand. There are butterflies and less attractive insects such as mosquitoes, ants and sand flies.

There is, however, a remarkable rich and colourful native bird life including the threatened St Vincent parrot. There are thought to

opposite, upper: The whaling boat at Friendship Bay, Bequia — one of the few places where whaling is still allowed

opposite, lower: Loading up for a scuba diving trip at Admiralty Bay, Bequia

be less than 500 of these attractive birds left in the wild, and the best chance of spotting them is to get up very early, and walk the nature trails in the Vermont area inland from Layou. The female is more brightly coloured than the male, and it has a brownish body with vivid blue wing tips and striking green, yellow and blue tail feathers. You can see what the bird looks like by visiting the aviary in the Botanic Gardens where there is a breeding programme underway.

Around Soufrière, you may spot the rare rufous-throated solitaire, and there are also mangrove cuckoos, humming birds, tanagers, ibis, mocking birds, herons, egrets and many others.

Offshore you may sight the Magnificent frigatebird, easily recognisable by its size, long black 7ft (2.1m) wingspan, forked tail and apparent effortless ability to glide on the winds. There are brown booby birds, named by sailors from the Spanish word for 'fool' because they were so easy to catch. Pelicans which look so ungainly on land, yet are so acrobatic in the air, are common, as are laughing gulls and royal terns. Several species of sandpiper can usually be seen scurrying around at the water's ege.

If you are really interested in bird watching pack a small pair of binoculars. The new mini-binoculars are ideal for island bird watching, because the light is normally so good that you will get a clear image despite the small object lens.

THE ISLANDS' FRUITS

Bananas are one of the island's most important exports, earning $176 million in 1994 thus their nickname 'green gold' — and they grow everywhere. There are three types of banana plant. The banana that is normally bought in supermarkets originated in Malaya and was introduced into the Caribbean in the early sixteenth century by the Spanish. The large bananas, or plantains, originally came from southern India, and are largely used in cooking; they are often fried and served as an accompaniment to fish and meat. The third variety is the red banana, which is not grown commercially, but which can be seen around the island. Most banana plantations cover only a few acres and are worked by the owner or tenant, although there are still some very large holdings. A banana produces a crop about every nine months, and each cluster of flowers grows into a hand of

— BEFORE YOU GO —

bananas. A bunch can contain up to twenty hands of bananas, with each hand having up to twenty individual fruit.

Although they grow tall, bananas are not trees but herbacious plants which die back each year. Once the plant has produced fruit, a shoot from the ground is cultivated to take its place, and the old plant dies. Bananas need a lot of attention, and island farmers will tell you that there are not enough hours in a day to do everything that needs to be done. The crop needs fertilising regularly, leaves need cutting back, and you will often see the fruit inside blue tinted plastic bags, which protect it from insect and bird attack, and speed up maturation.

Breadfruit was introduced to the Caribbean by Captain Bligh in 1793. He brought 1,200 breadfruit saplings from Tahiti aboard the *Providence*, and these were first planted in Jamaica and St Vincent, and then quickly spread throughout the islands. It was Bligh's attempts to bring in young breadfruit trees that led to the mutiny on the Bounty four years earlier. Bligh was given the command of the 215-ton *Bounty* in 1787 and was ordered to take the breadfruit trees from Tahiti to the West Indies where they were to be used to provide cheap food for the slaves. The ship had collected its cargo and had reached Tonga when the crew under Fletcher Christian mutinied. The crew claimed that Bligh's regime was too tyranical, and he and eighteen members of the crew who stayed loyal to him, were cast adrift in an open boat. The cargo of breadfruit was dumped overboard. Bligh, and in a remarkable feat of seamanship, navigated the boat for 3,600 miles (5,800km) until making landfall on Timor in the East Indies. Some authorities have claimed that it was the breadfruit tree cargo that sparked the mutiny, as each morning the hundreds of trees in their heavy containers had to be carried on deck, and then carried down into the hold at nightfall. It might have proved just too much for the already overworked crew.

Whatever the reason for the mutiny, the breadfruit is a cheap carbohydrate-rich food, although pretty tasteless when boiled. It is best eaten fried, baked or roasted over charcoal. The slaves did not like it at first, but the tree spread and can now be found almost everywhere. It has large dark, green leaves, and the large green fruits can weigh 10-12lb (4.5-5.4kg). The falling fruits explode with a loud bang and splatter its

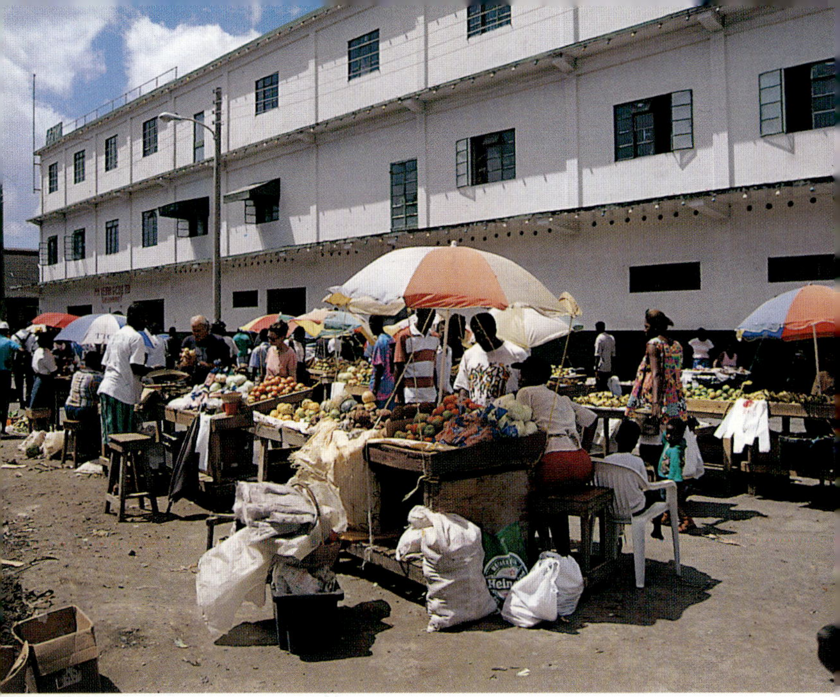

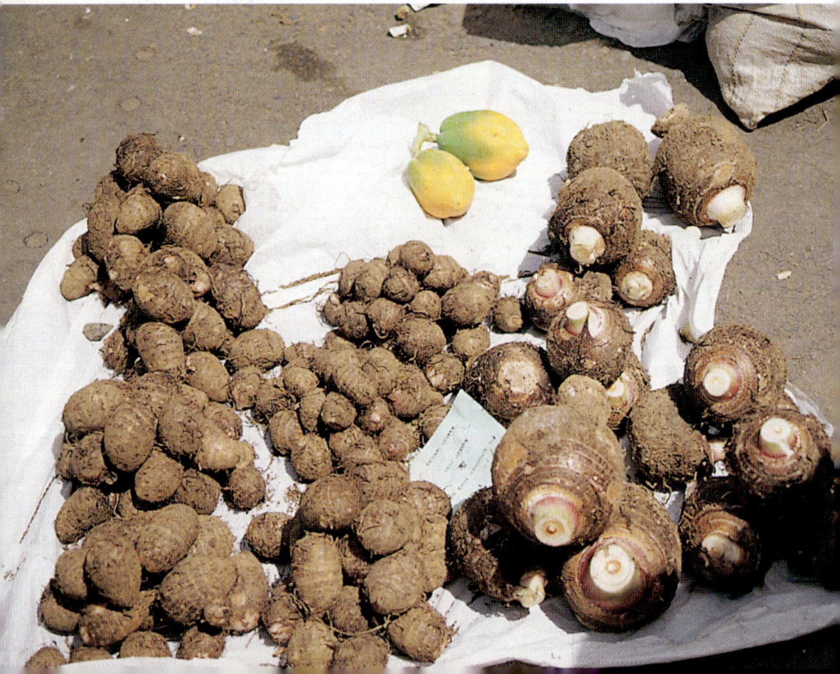

―――――――――――――― BEFORE YOU GO ――――――――――――――

SCUBA DIVING

St Vincent and the Grenadines offer some of the best diving waters in the world. The seas are warm and clear, the marine life is amazingly plentiful and diverse, and there are dives to suit everyone from the beginner to the most experienced. You can dive through teeming shoals of brightly coloured tiny fish, or rub shoulders with larger species such as barracuda, grouper, and parrot fish. And, if you have never dived before, there are qualified diving centres that can teach you everything you want to know.

The waters are rated so highly by divers because there is such a diversity of undersea experiences. You can snorkel in shallow, warm, crystal clear waters through shoals of rainbow coloured tropical fish, explore caves with lurking octopus and moray eels, and marvel at the colour and complexity of the extensive coral reefs. Another advantage of St. Vincent's coastline is its steeply sloping mountains which run straight into the sea, producing underwater cliffs, ideal for 'wall' dives. St. Vincent is also known for its black coral, which compared with many other Caribbean islands, lies in reasonably shallow waters so can be explored by divers of all capabilities. This hightly attractive coral is much prized for jewellery, but is protected around St. Vincent. The waters off St. Vincent also boast a number of species of fish not often found elsewhere; these include high hats, jack knife fish and spotted drums, and you will also see sea horses, blennys, angler fish and many others. The diving off the Grenadines is, if anything, even better than off St Vincent. Bequia and the Tobago Cays in particular, offer spectacular diving.

opposite: Kingstown market is a good place to see the wide range of locally-grown produce

pulpy contents over a large distance. It is said that no one goes hungry when the breadfruit is in season.

Calabash trees are native to the Caribbean and have huge gourd-like fruits which are very versatile when dried and cleaned. They can be used as water containers and bowls, bailers for boats, and as lanterns. Juice from the pulp is boiled into a concentrated syrup and used to treat coughs and colds, and the fruit is said to have many other medicinal uses.

Cocoa is another important crop, and its Latin name *theobroma* means 'food of the gods'. A cocoa tree can produce several thousand flowers a year, but only a fraction of these will develop into seed-bearing pods. It is the heavy orange pods that hang from the cocoa tree which contain the beans which contain the seeds that produce cocoa and chocolate. The beans, containing a sweet, white sap that protects the seeds, are split open and kept in trays to ferment. This process takes up to eight days and the seeds must be kept at a regular temperature to ensure that the right flavour and aroma develops. The seeds are then dried. In the old days people used to walk barefoot over the beans to polish them to enhance their appearance. Today, the beans are crushed to extract cocoa butter, and the remaining powder is cocoa. Real chocolate is produced by mixing cocoa powder, cocoa butter and sugar.

You can buy cocoa balls, like fat chcolate fingers, in the markets and these make a delicious drink. Each ball is the size of a large cherry. Simply dissolve the ball in a pan of boiling water, allow to simmer and then add sugar and milk or cream, for a rich chocolate drink. Each ball will make about four mugs of chocolate.

Coconut palms are everywhere and should be treated with caution. Anyone who has heard the whoosh of a descending coconut and leapt to safety, knows how scary the sound is. Those who did not hear the whoosh, presumably did not live to tell the tale. Actually, very few people do get injured by falling coconuts and that is a near miracle in view of the tens of thousands of palms all over the island, but it is not a good idea to picnic in a coconut grove!

Coconut trees are incredibly hardy, able to grow in sand and even when regularly washed by salty sea water. They can also survive long periods without rain. Their huge leaves, up to 20ft (6m) long in mature trees, drop down during dry spells so that a smaller surface area is exposed to the sun which reduces evaporation. Coconut palms can grow up to 80ft (24m) tall, and produce up to a hundred seeds a year. The seeds are the second largest in the plant kingdom, and these fall when ripe.

The coconut bought in shops is the seed with its layer of coconut surrounded by a hard shell. This has been removed from its surrounding layer of copra, a fibrous material, which is covered by a large green husk. The seed and protective coverings can weigh 30lb (14kg) and more. The seed and its casing is waterproof, drought proof and able to float, and this explains why coconut palms, which originated in the Pacific and Indian Oceans, are now found throughout the Caribbean — the seeds literally floated across the seas.

The coconut palm is extremely versatile. The leaves can be used as thatch for roofing, or cut into strips and woven into mat and baskets, while the husks yield coir, a fibre resistant to salt water and ideal for ropes, brushes and brooms. Green coconuts contain a delicious thirst-quenching 'milk', and the coconut 'meat' can be eaten raw, or baked in ovens for two days before being sent to processing plants where the oil is extracted. Coconut oil is used in cooking, soaps, synthetic rubber and even in hydraulic brake fluid.

As you travel around the island, you will see groups of men and women splitting the coconuts in half with machetes preparing them for the ovens. You might also see halved coconut shells spaced out on the corrugated tin roofs of some homes. These are being dried before being sold to the copra procressing plants.

Dasheen is one of the crops known as 'ground provisions' in the islands, the others being potatoes, yams, eddo and tannia. The last two are close relatives of dasheen, and all are members of the aroid family, some of the world's oldest cultivated crops. Dasheen with its 'elephant ear' leaves, and eddo grow from a corm which when boiled thoroughly can be used like potato, and the young leaves of either are used to make callaloo, a spinach-like soup. Both dasheen and eddo are thought to have come from China or Japan but tannia is native to the Caribbean, and its roots can be boiled, baked or fried.

Guava is common throughout the islands, and the aromatic, pulpy fruit is also a favourite with birds who then distribute its seeds. The fruit-bearing shrub can be seen on roadsides and in gardens, and it is used to make a wide range of products from jelly to 'cheese', a paste made by mixing the fruit with sugar. The fruit which ranges from a golf ball to a tennis ball in size, is a rich source of vitamin A and contains

St Vincent's lush vegetation includes colourful Jacaranda trees

much more vitamin C than citrus fruit.

Mango can be delicious, if somewhat messy to eat. It originally came from India but is now grown throughout the Caribbean and found wherever there are people. Young mangoes can be stringy and unappetising, but ripe fruit from mature trees which grow up to 50ft (15m) and more, are usually delicious, and can be

opposite, upper: Villa Beach on St Vincent, where you can get away from it all

opposite, lower: The remains of sugar cane crushing mills are a testimony to a once prosperous industry. One old mill at Layou on the west coast of St Vincent, still has its waterwheel, which was made in Glasgow and shipped across the Atlantic from Scotland

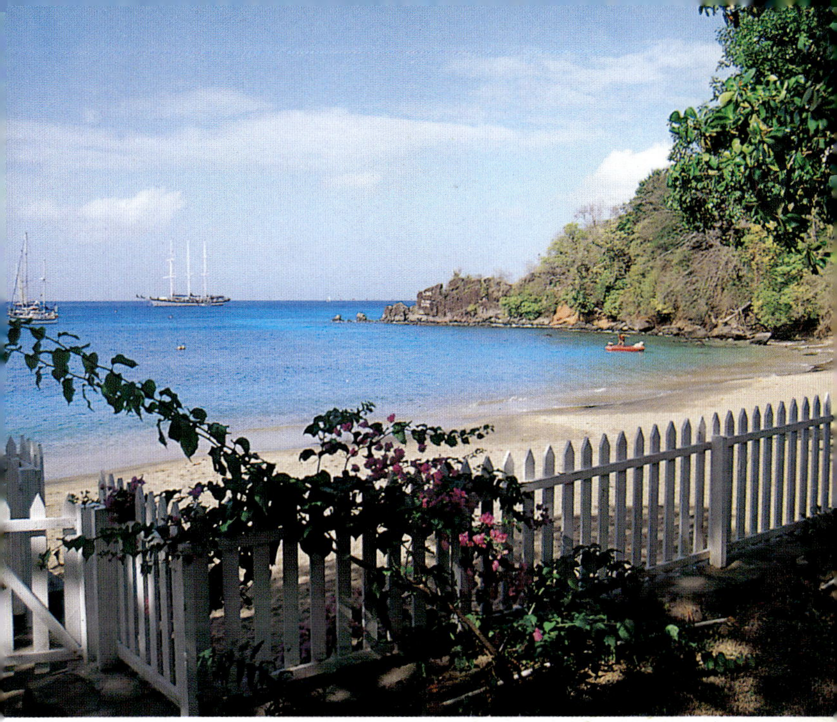

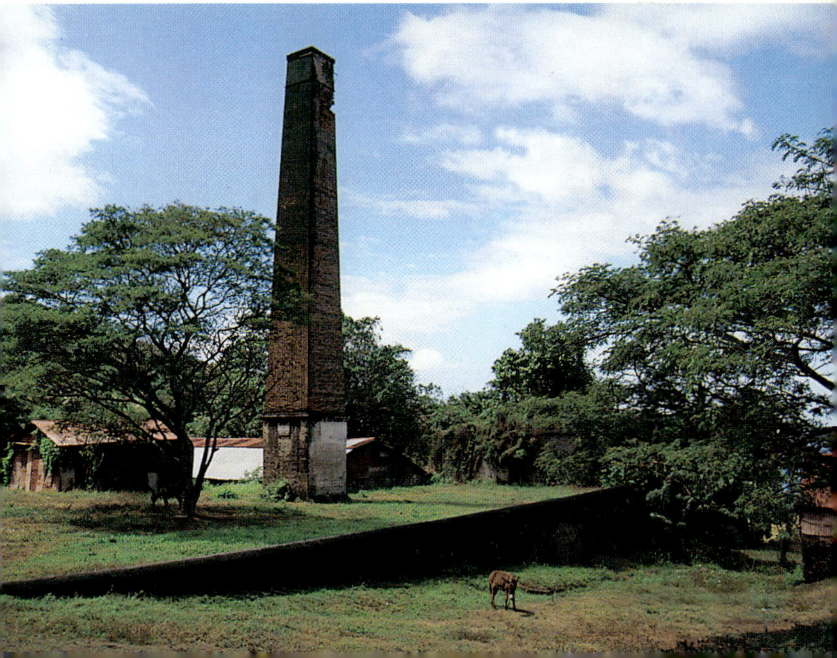

eaten raw or cooked. The juice is a great reviver in the morning, and the fruit is often used to make jams and other preserves. The wood of the mango is often used by boatbuilders.

Nutmeg trees are found on all the islands, although the price farmers get has crashed so much in recent years that it is sometimes not economic to gather the crop. The tree thrives in hilly, wet areas and the fruit is the size of a small tomato. The outer husk, which splits open while still on the tree, is used to make the very popular nutmeg jelly. Inside the seed is protected by a bright red casing which when dried and crushed, produces the spice mace. Finally, the dark outer shell of the seed is broken open to reveal the nutmeg which is dried and then ground into a powder, or sold whole so that it can be grated to add flavour to dishes.

Passion fruit is not widely grown but it can usually be bought at the market. The pulpy fruit contains hundreds of tiny seeds, and many people prefer to press the fruit and drink the juice. It is also commonly used in fruit salads, sherbets and ice creams.

Pawpaw trees are also found throughout the island and are commonly grown in gardens. The trees are prolific fruit producers but grow so quickly that the fruit soon becomes difficult to gather. The large, juicy melon-like fruits are eaten fresh, pulped for juice or used locally to make jams, preserves and ice cream. They are rich sources of vitamin A and C. The leaves and fruit contain an enzyme which tenderises meat, and tough joints cooked wrapped in pawpaw leaves or covered in slices of fruit, usually taste like much more expensive cuts. The same enzyme, papain, is also used in chewing gum, cosmetics, the tanning industry and, somehow, in making wool shrink resistant. A tea made from unripe fruit is said to be good for lowering high blood pressure.

Pigeon peas are widely cultivated and can be found in many back gardens. The plants are very hardy and drought resistant, and are prolific yields of peas which can be eaten fresh or dried and used in soups and stews.

Pineapples were certainly grown in the Caribbean by the time Columbus arrived, and were probably brought from South America by the Amerindians. The fruit is slightly smaller than the Pacific pineapple, but the flavour more intense.

Sugar cane is no longer grown commercially but can still be seen growing. The canes can grow up to 12ft (3.6m) tall and after cutting, the canes had to be crushed to extract the sugary juice. Most estates had their own sugar mill powered by waterwheels or windmills. The remains of many of these mills can still be seen around the island, and much of the original mchinery, mostly made in Britain, is still in place. After extraction, the juice was boiled until the sugar crystalised. The mixture remaining was molasses and this was used to produce rum.

Sugar apple is a member of the annona fruit family, and grows wild and in gardens throughout the islands. The small, soft sugar apple fruit can be peeled off in strips when ripe, and is like eating thick apple sauce. They are eaten fresh or used to make sherbet or drinks. Soursop, is a member of the same family, and its spiny fruits can be seen in hedgerows and gardens. They are eaten fresh or used for preserves, drinks and ice cream.

FOOD

Dining out in the Caribbean offers the chance to experiment with all sorts of unusual spices, vegetables and fruits, with creole and island dishes, and, of course, rum punches and other exotic cocktails.

Many hotels have a tendency to offer buffet dinners or barbecues, but even these can be interesting and tasty affairs.

Eating out is generally very relaxed, and few restaurants have a strict dress code, although most people like to wear something a little smarter at dinner after a day on the beach or out sightseeing.

Lunches are best eaten at beach cafés which usually offer excellent barbecued fresh fish and conch — which often appears on menus as lambi (not to be confused with lamb). Lobster and crab are also widely available. Dishes are mostly served with local vegetables such as fried plantain, cassava and yam, and fresh fruit such as pineapple, mango, golden apple or papaya, makes an ideal and light dessert.

There is an enormous choice when it comes to dinner. Starters include traditional Caribbean dishes such as Christophene and coconut soup, and Callaloo soup made from the leaves of dasheen, a spinach-like vegetable. There is also a strong French tradition with *soupe Germou* made from pumpkin and garlic, and *pouile dudon*, a chicken

PEPPER SAUCE — HOT OR HOTTER?

Another note of warning: on most tables you will find a bottle of pepper sauce. It usually contains a blend of several types of hot pepper, spices and vinegar, and should be treated cautiously. Try a little first before splashing it all over your food, as these sauces range from hot to unbearable.

If you want to make your own hot pepper sauce, take four ripe hot peppers, one teaspoon each of oil, ketchup and vinegar and a pinch of salt, blend together into a liquid, and bottle.

St Vincent's flowers are a feast for the eyes

Relaxing with a cool drink at the Plantation Hotel on Bequia

stew with coconut and molasses. Fish and clam chowders are also popular starters. Try heart of palm, excellent fresh shrimps or scallops, smoked kingfish wrapped in crepes or crab backs, succulent land crab meat sauteed with breadcrumbs and seasoning, and served restuffed in the shell. It is much sweeter than the meat of sea crabs.

The fish is generally excellent, and do not be alarmed if you see dolphin on the menu. It is not the protected species of marine mammal, but a solid, close-textured flat-faced fish called dorado, which is delicious. There is also snapper, tuna, lobster, swordfish, baby squid and mussels.

Try seafood jambalaya, chunks

of lobster, shrimps and ham served on a bed of braised seasoned rice; shrimp creole, with fresh shrimp sauted in garlic butter and parsley and served with tomatoes; or fish creole, with fresh fish steaks cooked in a spicy onion, garlic and tomato sauce and served with rice and fried plaintain. Other island specialities include sauted scallops with ginger, curried fish steaks lightly fried with a curry sauce and served with sliced bananas, cucumber, fresh coconut and rice.

It seems such a waste to travel to the Caribbean and eat burgers and steaks, especially when there are many much more exciting meat dishes available.

You could try curried chicken served in a coconut shell, curried goat, gingered chicken with mango and spices; Caribbean souse, with cuts of lean pork marinated with shredded cucumber, onions, garlic, lime juice and pepper sauce.

For vegetarians there are excellent salads, stuffed breadfruit, callaloo bake, stuffed squash and pawpaw, baked sweet potato and yam casserole.

For dessert, try fresh fruit salad, or one of the exotically flavoured ice creams. There are also banana fritters and banana flambe, coconut cheesecake and tropical fruit sorbets.

Most menus and dishes are self explanatory, but one or two things are worth bearing in mind. When green fig appears on the menu, it usually means green banana, which is peeled and boiled as a vegetable. Salt fish used to be salted cod, but now it can be any fish.

On the buffet table, you will often see a dish called pepper pot. This is usually a hot, spicy meat and vegetable stew to which may be added small flour dumplings and shrimps.

There are wonderful breads in the Caribbean, and you should try them if you get the chance. There are banana and pumpkin breads, and delicious cakes such as coconut loaf cake, guava jelly cookies and rum cake.

Do not be afraid to eat out. Food is often prepared in front of you, and there are some great snacks available from island eateries. Try deep fried cakes of dough called floats, or saltfish or corned beef fritters, or coconut patties.

You must try roti, an East Indian creation, which is available almost everywhere. It is a paper-thin dough wrapped round a spicy, hot curry mixture, and contains beef, chicken, vegetables or fish.

The chicken roti often contains bones which some people like to chew on, so be warned.

DRINKS

Rum is the Caribbean drink. There are almost as many rums in the West Indies as their are malt whiskies in Scotland, and there is an amazing variety of strength, colour and quality. The finest rums are best drunk on the rocks, but if you want to capture a bit of the Caribbean spirit, have a couple of rum punches.

To make Plantation Rum Punch, thoroughly mix three ounces of rum, with one ounce of lime juice and one teaspoon of honey, then pour over crushed ice, and add a pinch of freshly grated nutmeg.

Most hotels and bars also offer a wide range of cocktails both alcoholic, usually very strong, and non-alcoholic. The good local beer, drunk cold and from the bottle, is the most popular drink, and wine, where available, is often expensive because of taxes, and the choice limited.

Tap water is safe to drink, as are ice cubes made from it. Mineral and bottled water is widely available, as are soft drinks.

Note: While many of the restaurants do offer excellent service, time does not always have the same urgency as it does back home, and why should it after all, as you are on holiday. Relax, enjoy a drink, the company and the surroundings and do not worry if things take just a little longer, the wait is generally worth it.

The old fort, Admiralty Bay, Bequia

Touring & Exploring St Vincent

GETTING AROUND ST VINCENT

Many hotels and guest houses provide courtesy transport to and from the airports, and taxis are a good alternative if you do not want to drive a hire car after a long flight.

By Hire Car

Car or jeep hire is the best option if you are planning to spend several days on the island and want to explore. If you plan only an occasional trip, use taxis or the island's 'bus' service. All towns and villages are connected to the

Kingstown harbour

main highways even though these side roads may be rough and potholed, they are usually passable with care.

By Taxi

Taxis are cheap and plentiful and can be ordered by telephone from your hotel or picked up at taxi ranks at the airport or in Kingstown. All taxi fares are fixed by the Government, but prices are negotiable if you want to hire a taxi for sightseeing tours or long periods. Taxi drivers make excellent guides, and vehicles can be hired by the trip, the hour or day for sightseeing tours, but make sure the price is agreed first, and you know which currency you are paying in.

Expect to pay around EC$40 an hour if hiring a taxi for a tour. As an example of fixed fares, it is EC$15 between Kingstown and the airport, EC$10 from Kingstown to Fort Charlotte, and EC$35 from Kingstown to Mesopotamia. A full list of fares is available from the tourist office and the dispatcher at the airport.

By Minibus

Minibuses, privately owned Japanese vans, ply the main routes on the island, generally carrying up to ten passengers. They offer a fun way of getting around, provided you know where they are going, and they offer a great way of getting to know the islanders. Always check that the bus is heading in your direction before getting on. Most drivers have adopted flamboyant names which are boldly printed across the front of the vehicle, and music is generally played at near-deafening volumes inside. There is no scheduled bus service, although drivers have their own routes and follow their own timetables. Buses leave Kingstown from around the market area, and en route can usually be flagged down if there are empty seats. At peak times, the buses are often full and you just have to be patient until the next one with empty seats comes along. Most buses bring people into Kingstown to work, and run until they have taken them back again. They tend not to run in the evenings and are scarce on Sundays. Fares are again fixed by the Government and you can flag them down on the road. Typical fares from Kingstown are: EC$2 to Layou, EC$2.50 to Mesopotamia, EC$4 to Georgetown, and EC$5 to Sandy Bay.

By Boat

There are regular ferry services between St Vincent and Bequia,

― TOURING & EXPLORING ST VINCENT ―

and between St Vincent and the other Grenadines as far south as Union Island. All ferries leave Kingstown from the Grenadines Ferry Jetty, to the south of the deep water dock.

There are three ferries on the St Vincent-Bequia run. Between Monday and Friday and Sunday, the first boat from St Vincent to Bequia sails at 9am. On Saturday the first boat to Bequia does not leave until 12.30pm. The last ferry sails at 7pm each evening. From Bequia to St Vincent, the first ferry leaves at 6.30am between Monday and Saturday, and at 7.30am on Sunday. The last ferry leaves at 5pm every night. The ferries usually leave on time, and it is a good idea to arrive early. Fares are collected on board and are EC$10 for a single ticket Monday to Saturday, and EC$12 on Sunday. The crossing takes about one hour, and be warned, it can be quite rough, especially when one leaves the lee of the island and the Atlantic breakers hit the ferry side on.

The mail boat MV *Snapper* sails from St Vincent at around 10am three times a week — Monday, Thursday and Saturday, and calls at Bequia, Canouan, Mayreau and Union Island. The trip from St Vincent to Union Island including stops at the other ports of call takes just over 5 hours depending on the seas. The ferry returns on Tuesday and Friday after an all-night stop-over on Union Island sailing at 7am and arriving back in St Vincent at noon. On Saturday the ferry docks for only less than two hours before sailing at 5.30pm for St Vincent, arriving at 10.30pm. Always ring to confirm times of sailings.

MV *Snapper* offers a great way of visiting the islands and even if you take the Saturday sailing, and only spend an hour or so on Union Island, you will get some fabulous views as you cruise through the Grenadines. The fare from St Vincent to Bequia is EC$10 (EC$12 at night and weekends), to Canouan EC$13, to Mayreau EC$15 and Union Island EC$20.

There are a number of companies offering boat trips or vessels for charter, either 'bareboat' in which you provide provisions and crew the boat yourself, or with a full crew provided.

By Air

Liat and Mustique Airways fly scheduled services in the islands. LIAT offers a number of sightseeing flights and day tours from St Vincent, and both Mustique Airways and SVG Air are available for charter.

A boat trip from Kingstown on the island of St Vincent, makes a relaxing short cruise with fabulous views of the Grenadines

opposite: The ornate tower of St Mary's Roman Catholic Cathedral, Kingstown

CARNIVAL

Carnival takes place over several days at the beginning of July and Kingstown is where most of the celebrations take place. There are costume parades and children's carnival, competitions to find the best steelband, Calypso King, and the King and Queen of the Bands. Throughout Carnival there are parties, jump-ups and street celebrations, and the grand finale is the Street Parade through the streets of Kingstown. Carnival has an atmosphere and vibrancy all of its own, and something you just have to experience for yourself.

TOURING & EXPLORING ST VINCENT

ST VINCENT

The island of St Vincent is small and fun to explore although most trips take longer than you would imagine from the map. There are about 300 miles of road, but some are only suitable for four-wheel drive vehicles.

Although Richmond is only 15 miles or so by road up the west coast from Kingstown, you need to plan on spending at least three hours getting there and back, and much more if you are going to stop several times on the way to take photographs, do a little exploring, perhaps have a swim or have something to eat and drink.

While most of the west coast and all the south and east coast are accessible by vehicle, much of the interior is not, and the only way in is on foot. There are many beautiful walks, however, and these offer you the best chance to see natural St Vincent at its best.

Almost all the place names on St Vincent reflect the island's past, either British, French or Amerindian. For many years virtually the whole island was divided up between various estates, and most of the villages that developed on them, still carry the names of the former estate owners.

KINGSTOWN

This is a typical West caribbean waterfront town, bustling, noisy, lots of hooting traffic, with a busy market which also serves as the main bus station.

It is a small, compact town and easy to explore on foot. There is lots of modernisation and rebuilding going on, such as the new Government and banking offices which include the tourist board, on the waterfront, but there are still some fine old buildings, many of them dating back to the nineteenth century. There are old cobblestones and tiny alleys, and the main streets have sidewalks often with overhanging upper storey balconies supported by wooden pillars, which offer pedestrians some protection from both sun and rain.

The heart of downtown Kingstown, however, is still concentrated in a dozen or so blocks between Upper and Lower Bay Streets which run along the water front and Tyrell, Grenville and Halifax Streets which together form a continuous road and run parallel with them. Traffic has become so busy at peak periods that even traffic control have had to be installed.

There are lots of shops and stores to browse through offering a wide range of goods from duty free items to local handicrafts and batik wear to preserves, and the old fruit and vegetable market and the new fish market are a must.

Kingstown has a wonderful natural harbour with deep water facilities and a new container park, and a new container port at Campden Park just up the coast is now operational. Work is well under way for a new cruise ship facility in Kingstown.

Much of the land between Lower Bay Street and the water line has been reclaimed from the sea.

A Walking Tour of Kingstown

The ferry boat jetty makes a good starting point for a walking tour of Kingstown, and it is a lively place as the ferries load up and disgorge their passengers, and the schooners take on cargo for delivery to the other Grenadine islands. Taxis and minibuses are not allowed to drive up to the ferries which dock at the end of the jetty, so they reverse up with remarkable skill, avoiding the people, other vehicles and piles of luggage and freight along the way. Many of the warehouses were built from bricks brought out from England as ballast in the vessels which returned laden with molasses and sugar.

From the ferry jetty turn left on to **Grenadines Wharf**, with its many old warehouses and nineteenth-century buildings, including an old arrowroot store. The road then runs into Upper Bay Street. The new multi-storey building on the waterfront beyond the deep water wharf, are the Govenment Offices. It also houses the tourist board. Just beyond this is the imposing red-roofed, stone police headquarters built in 1875, with its immaculate officers on duty outside, and then the new fish market and bus station. Take a look at the historic Cobblestone Inn on Bay Street. The inn was built in 1813 and King JaJa of Opobo in Africa is said to have stayed here in 1888 while in exile. Almost across the road is the site where Captain Uring landed in 1723 in an unsuccessful attempt to settle *Oooshegunny*, as Kingstown was then known.

Retrace your steps and turn left into South River. On the corner of South River and Upper Bay Street is Noah's Arkade which offers books and detailed maps, as well as island handicrafts and souvenirs.

The LIAT offices are at the top of South River Road. At the junction with Halifax Street turn left past the General Post Office and many of the banks, including

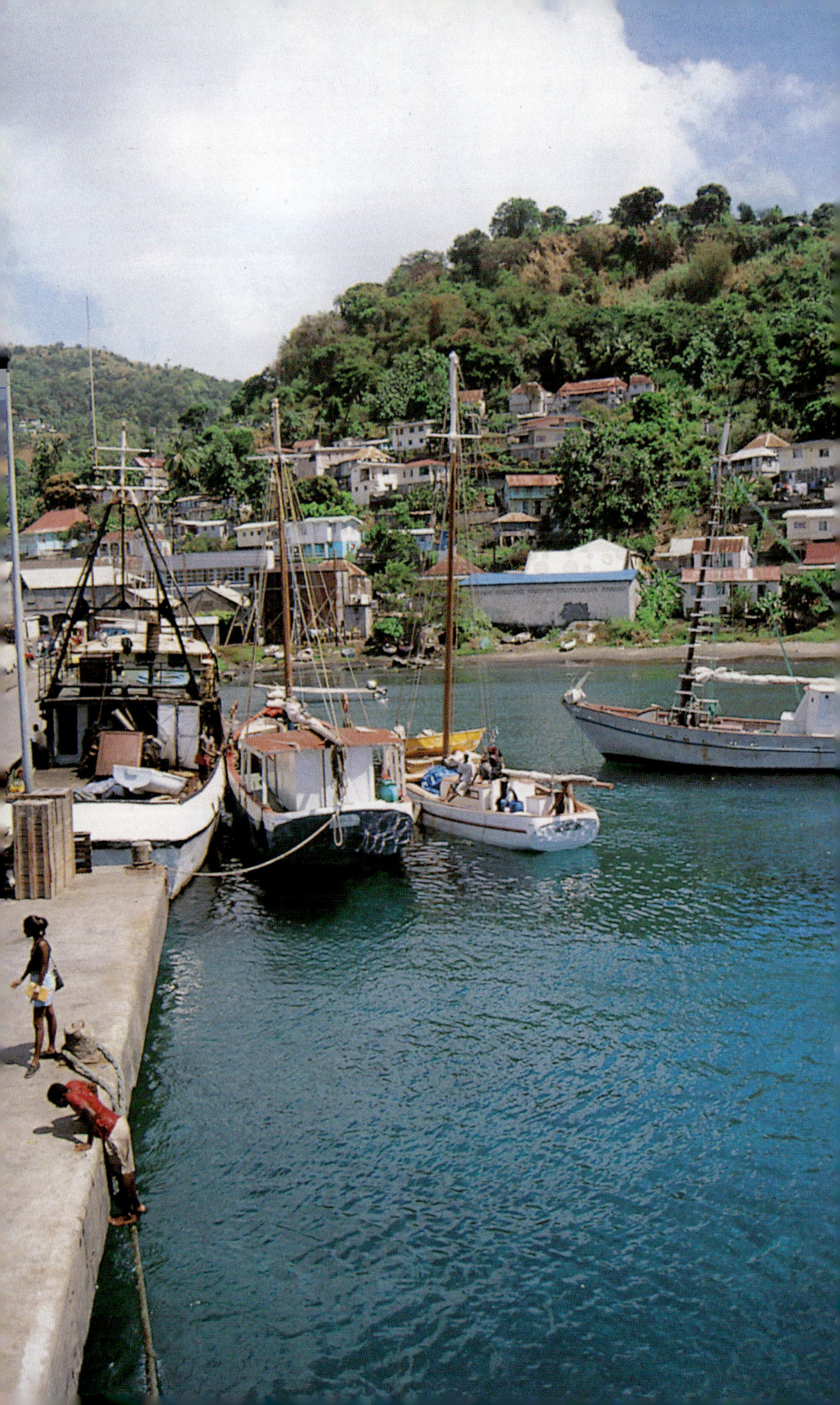

TOURING & EXPLORING ST VINCENT

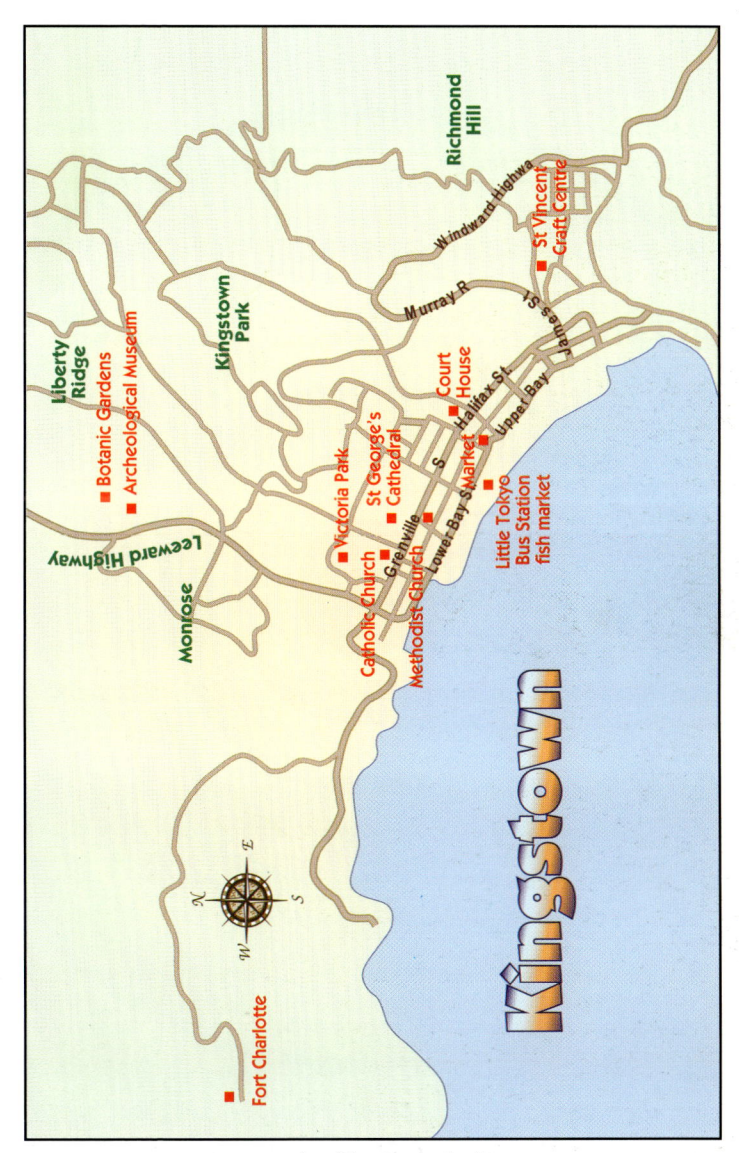

opposite: Kingstown harbour

Barclays, and the offices of Cable and Wireless on your right, with the **Court House**, built from local stone in 1798, just across the junction from Hillsborough Street. The state's fifteen members of parliament also meet in the Law Courts. Turn left into Hillsborough Street past the Cenotaph for the **Market**, which lies between Hillsborough and Bedford Streets. The market offers the opportunity to see just what a wide variety of produce is grown on the island, and items on sale such as preserves, spices and products made from them make excellent gifts. The produce is often displayed on blankets laid on the ground, and protected from the sun by bright, multi-coloured golf-style umbrellas. The jovial women selling the produce sit on boxes or similar, shouting bits of news and gossip to each other, and trying to persuade passers-by to buy their wares.

Around the market there are also plenty of opportunities to sample local dishes from the snackettes and stalls.

From the market, take Lower Bay Street along the waterfront past the new fish market built largely with Japanese financing — thus the area's local name of **'Little Tokyo'** — to the Philatelic Bureau, where you can buy the island's very colourful commemorative stamps, and then back track a little to take Higginson Street up to Grenville Street. If you fancy a spot of lunch, pop in to Sid's on Grenville Street. It is upstairs, packed with cricket photographs, many featuring the owner, and the two televisions are usually tuned in to cricket if there is a match on. The pub offers excellent West Indian food, and there are special dishes of the day which appear only minutes after ordering. And, if you are thirsty, order a pitcher of draught beer. It is a very lively place at most times of the day, good food and great value. Aggie's just up the street, and also upstairs, is famous for its seafood in spicy Creole sauces, and its traditional scouse.

On the corner of Higginson and Grenville Streets is the **Methodist Church**. Methodist missionaries bought a small plot of land on which stood an old church, from the Catholic authorities in 1790, and with money later raised largely by freed slaves, a new church was built and dedicated in 1841. The belfry was not added until 1907. The interior is very light and there is a very elaborate and large pipe organ.

Turn left into Grenvile Street and almost opposite is the **Anglican Cathedral of St George**, with its striking clock tower. The nave and lower parts of the tower date from about 1820, and the church was largely built from money raised by the sale of Carib lands after the Second Carib War. There is a fine Georgian galleried interior, and some beautiful stained glass windows, three by Kempe on the east wall, and the large one on the south is in Munich Glass. The two transepts were added in the 1880s and are pure Victorian.

One window shows the famous 'Red Angel'. This stained glass window was commissioned by Queen Victoria for St Paul's Cathedral in London, and was supposed to depict an angel dressed in white. The artist, however, misunderstood and portrayed the angel in red garments. The Queen refused to have the window installed, and it was hidden away in the basement of the cathedral. It was here that Bishop Jackson spotted it, and asked Dean Inge of St Paul's if he could take it back with him to St Vincent for his cathedral. The chandelier in the cathedral was also originally destined to be hung elsewhere. It was bound for Brazil but the ship carrying it, grounded off St Vincent, and the chandelier was saved for the church. Beneath the chandelier lies a stone plaque to Major Leith.

A little further down the road, just after North River Road, is the very unusual **St Mary's Roman Catholic Cathedral**. The first church on the site was built during 1823-8, but extended and the steeple and sanctuary added in 1877, and enlarged again in 1891. In the late 1930s and early 1940s it was totally renovated by the Flemish Dominican Charles Verbeke. This cycle of building has resulted in a mix of architectural styles, although the building is still largely Romanesque with heavy Gothic overtones, and it has a very ornate interior. Next door is the Cathedral School and Presbytery.

Take the next right into North River Road to arrive at **Victoria Park**.

If you are feeling energetic you can then take the road west out of town to Fort Charlotte, or take the Leeward Highway, past the Kingstown General Hospital, to the Botanical Gardens and Pre-Columbian Museum.

OTHER PLACES TO VISIT

Fort Charlotte stands 600ft (183m) above the sea on the promontory known as Berkshire Hill, just west of Kingstown and with great views over the town

ST VINCENT BOTANICAL GARDENS

St Vincent's Botanical Gardens, started in 1765, are the oldest in the western world. They originally covered 30 acres and today, 20 glorious acres remain, which are well tended and contain a wealth of tropical plants, shrubs and trees. The gardens have always been involved in conservation work, and one of their original functions was to grow herbs and plants which could be used for medicinal purposes. It was also a Way Station for the Royal Botanic Gardens at Kew in England, acting as a quarantine post. Plants destined for Kew would be planted here and their growth monitored to ensure they were disease free before being sent on to England.

The gardens contain many rare species, such as the Bermuda Cedar, now extinct in their natural habitat. At the far end of the gardens, there is a massive breadfruit tree. The plaque beneath states that the tree was grown from one of the original plants brought to St Vincent by Captain Bligh on HMS *Providence* in 1793.

There is also a fine specimen of the Soufriere Tree, the last one if its species in the world. It was one of several brought from the slopes of the volcano and planted in the gardens in 1812, but it is the only one surviving today. All the trees in the wild were wiped out following the various eruptions of Soufriere over the past 150 years. The Soufriere flower is the national flower.

The Century Alm gets its name because it reputedly blooms once every hundred years or so, producing massive canopies of flowers for five or six months, and then it dies. The Julie Mango which grows in St Vincent, and is displayed in the garden, is the juiciest of all the mango varieties, and has less fibre. The Sausage Tree with its huge black pea pods yields cascara, and is a powerful laxative, and the massive Pandamis, a native of Madagascar and member of the pineapple family, has an incredible aerial root system. The Red Ti plants are the same as those used to make Hawaiian grass skirts, and the grass when moistened and placed on the forehead, is said to cure headaches.

There are always many flowers in bloom, and the gardens are laid out in such a way that there are frequent new vistas and new surprises. The scene looking across the water-lily pond to the gazebo behind is a much photographed one, and the gardens, especially Hibiscus Alley with fifty different varieties on display, are a favourite location for newlyweds to have their wedding photographs taken.

African Tulip Tree in the St Vincent Botanical Gardens, just north of Kingstown

and surrounding countryside. It is now used as a coastguard lookout. You can see how the town has expanded with the new high rise government office buildings by the waterfront. Inland and to the south, densely wooded hills rise above Kingstown with colourful homes scattered among the trees. There are the big Colonial homes in Kingstown Vale which used to be surrounded by large gardens, but pressure for new building land has reduced them considerably. You can also see the new homes of the Grenadian rich, higher up the hillsides, and with their own magnificent views. From the fort, named after George III's queen, there are also views along the coast and across to the Grenadines to the south. You can walk or drive to the fort and it is a great place for either a lunchtime picnic, or to watch a spectacular sunset out to sea. The walk to the fort, uphill all the way, will take between 30 and 40 minutes — but at least it is downhill on the way back.

The fort was started by the English shortly after the island was ceded to Britain by the Treaty of Paris in 1763, and construction continued until 1806 when the lighthouse was added. There is a steep road up to the fort and you enter through a massive arch. The fort used to have formidable armaments with thirty-four guns, most of them pointing inland, but it never saw action. In fact, the only record of any trouble involving the fort was when a soldier got involved in a fight with an officer and killed him. The soldier was tried, convincted and hanged in the fort. Today only a handful of cannon remain. The fort's bakery used to be manned by prison labour and supplied bread to the island's hospital, prison and other public institutions. The former officers' quarters have been turned into a small pictorial museum, with a number of paintings by Lindsay (Linzee) Prescott of historical scenes from Black Carib history.

The **St Vincent Botanical Gardens** are a delight. Admission is free and you can spend hours wandering around the beautiful grounds. They are on the western outskirts of town and as you arrive at the entrance you will be descended on by guides offering to show you round, but do not let this put you off. It really does pay to have your own conducted tour as the guides are generally very well informed, and they will make sure you do not miss a thing. While their botanical knowledge is not always totally accurate, their anecdotes are interesting and amusing, they know where to take the best photographs, and they will explain how the various fruits that are in season are processed and used. If you decide on a conducted tour, it is best to agree a fee before setting off, but you can walk around on your own if you prefer. The gardens are open from dawn to dusk.

The gardens are the oldest in the western hemisphere, and were founded in 1765 by General Robert Melville, Governor-in-Chief of the Windward Federation, on land donated by Governor Sir William Young, after whom Young Island is named. The gardens originally covered 30 acres and planting was largely under the direction of Dr George Young, a principal medical officer and keen horticulturalist, who was appointed the first curator. In 1779 St Vincent was taken over by the French and came under the control of General de Bouille, the Commander-in-Chief of forces in Martinique. He was also a keen botanist and became a close friend of Dr Young.

Dr Alexander Anderson took over as curator in 1783 and although St Vincent had reverted to British control, he maintained links with de Brouille who in 1791 sent specimens of black pepper and nutmeg from French Guyana.

In 1828 three acres were set aside for Government House, and although the gardens then went through a period of decline, they have been well restored.

In the far corner of the gardens, there is an aviary where you can see the endangered St Vincent parrot. The aviary is running a breeding programme to release young birds back into the wild.

The Governor General's Residence stands in splendid isolation overlooking the Botanical Gardens. There is a private gateway leading from the gardens up to the house, built in 1886 and set in its own landscaped gardens.

The **Archaeological Museum** is in the Botanical Gardens, in what used to be the Gardens Curator's House, built in 1891. The museum specialises in the pre-Columbian history of the island, and the fascinating exhibits were largely put together by Dr Kirby, who is the curator. The museum is tiny and there are too many exhibits to be displayed properly, and the hope is that all can be moved into the old Carnegie Library on Granby Street in downtown Kingstown, where they would have the space they deserve. Outside the museum there are a number of large artifacts, as well as some of the plants that would have been grown by the early

Layou, on the west coast

opposite: Barrouallie

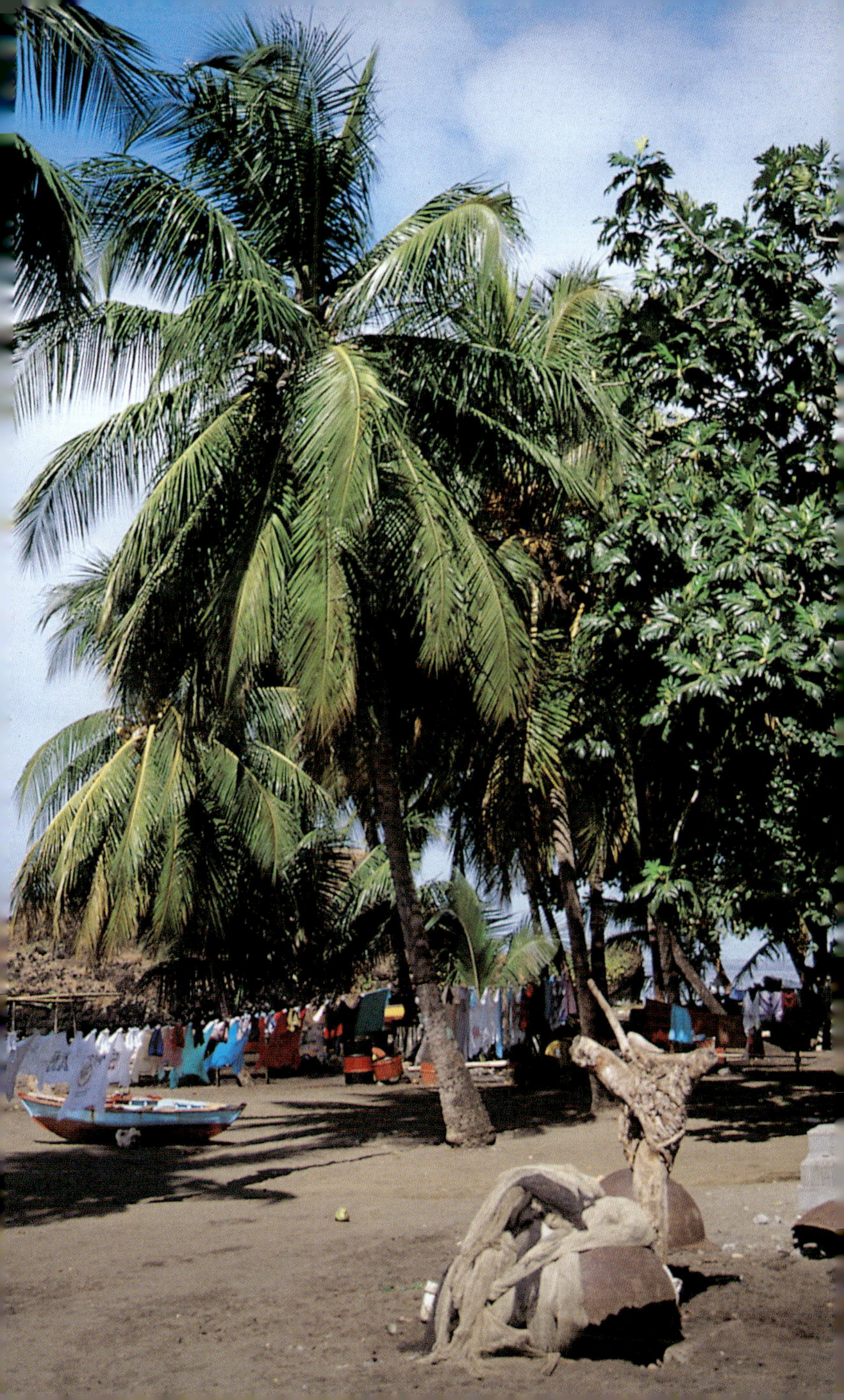

Arawaks and Caribs. Inside, there are maps showing how these early Amerindians moved through the eastern Caribbean, colonising most of the islands. The display cabinets contain Arawak and Carib artifacts, stone axes, pottery and jewellery and illustrate how styles and artistic skills changed through the different periods of civilisation. Other exhibits include a huge bathhead pot and dug-out canoe. The museum is worthy of a visit, and even more so when Dr Kirby is in attendance. There is a small admission charge.

After leaving, take time to look at Isaac's House, near the entrance. The house was built at the beginning of the twentieth century for Sydney Barber Isaac, a Kingstown magistrate.

The **St Vincent Craftsmen's Centre** is on the outskirts of the town and you get there by taking the airport road. It is a short walk from the centre of the town and clearly signposted. The centre used to be a market where sea island cotton was bought and sold. Today, you not only have the chance to buy some wonderful items of island handicraft, you can often watch the artisans at work, perhaps weaving straw, creating jewellery, moulding clay or sculpting in wood, coconut and other materials. Of particular interest are the hand-made West Indian dolls dressed in traditional costumes.

THE WEST COAST

Kingstown to Richmond & Petit Bordel Bay

This road leads along the coast through several small, picturesque fishing villages, which offer some of the island's best scuba diving.

The Leeward Highway starts in Kingstown and runs past the Botanical Gardens, and up over the hill, from the summit of which there are fine views back over Kingstown and ahead to Campden Park Bay.

The road is narrow in places and one should drive with care, but there is no need to rush.

The road runs inland from **Petit Byahaut**, a 50-acre valley which runs inland from a fabulous secluded bay, and can only be reached by boat. The small valley has a wealth of wildlife, and you can find mango, sugar apple, guava, banana, soursop, sapodilla, citrus and coconut. There are flowering plants such as hibiscus, frangipani, morning glory and allamanda, and the turquoise waters washing up on the white sand beach, teem with brightly-

TOURING & EXPLORING ST VINCENT

coloured tropical fish. As you can only get in by boat, this is one of the most exclusive get-aways on the island, providing comfortable accommodation, candlelit dinners and the morning chorus for your alarm call.

At **Buccament** there is a government banana collecting and packing station in the village, and beside the road which runs through the Cane Grove Estate to the sea, are a number of rocks bearing petroglyphs, carved many centuries ago by Arawak or Carib Indians.

At Cane Grove Estate there is also a feeder road running inland. It follows the river along the Buccament Valley through Peniston to **Vermont**. At the head of the valley there are nature trails up into the rain forest. Here you are dwarfed by massive trees with canopies blocking out the light and draped with huge hanging vines. There are some open areas where you may spot birds, although they are usually heard rather than seen, and benches are provided. You may be lucky and spot the rare St Vincent parrot, and the best chance for this is first thing in the morning shortly after dawn, or late in the afternoon when they come out to feed. Like most birds and animals, they tend to shelter during the hottest parts of the day. Another secretive rare bird that is sometimes spotted is the Whisting Warbler, also only found on St Vincent. More common species here include the red capped green tanager, cocoa thrush, crested hummingbird and black hawk.

There are two well-marked trails, which split just after the bridge not far from the start. The longer trail takes two hours and the shorter one about half this, although there is so much to see and spot along both that you could spend the whole day here, enjoying a picnic lunch into the bargain. A short distance downstream from the bridge at Table Rock, there are pools and small waterfalls.

Just inland from Layou is the Emerald Valley Hotel and Casino, the only casino on the island.

If you continue up the coast you arrive at **Layou**, a pretty fishing village with colourful fishing boats pulled up on the beach under palm trees. The village, which has a small police station, is also noted for its Crucifix with a Black Christ, which is in the cemetery by the church. The village has lots of small houses, many with ornate balconies, and it is fun to watch the fishermen at work.

Most of the open boats fish

using nets with one end secured on land. The boats, with four rowers and two men feeding out the rest of the net, make their way out into the bay and then make a loop which brings them back to the beach. The other end of the net is handed ashore, and then it is all hands to the ropes as the net, hopefully with a full catch of

The origin of the ancient carved rock, or petroglyph, is proudly explained by a pupil at the school in Barrouallie

opposite: Wallilabou Bay

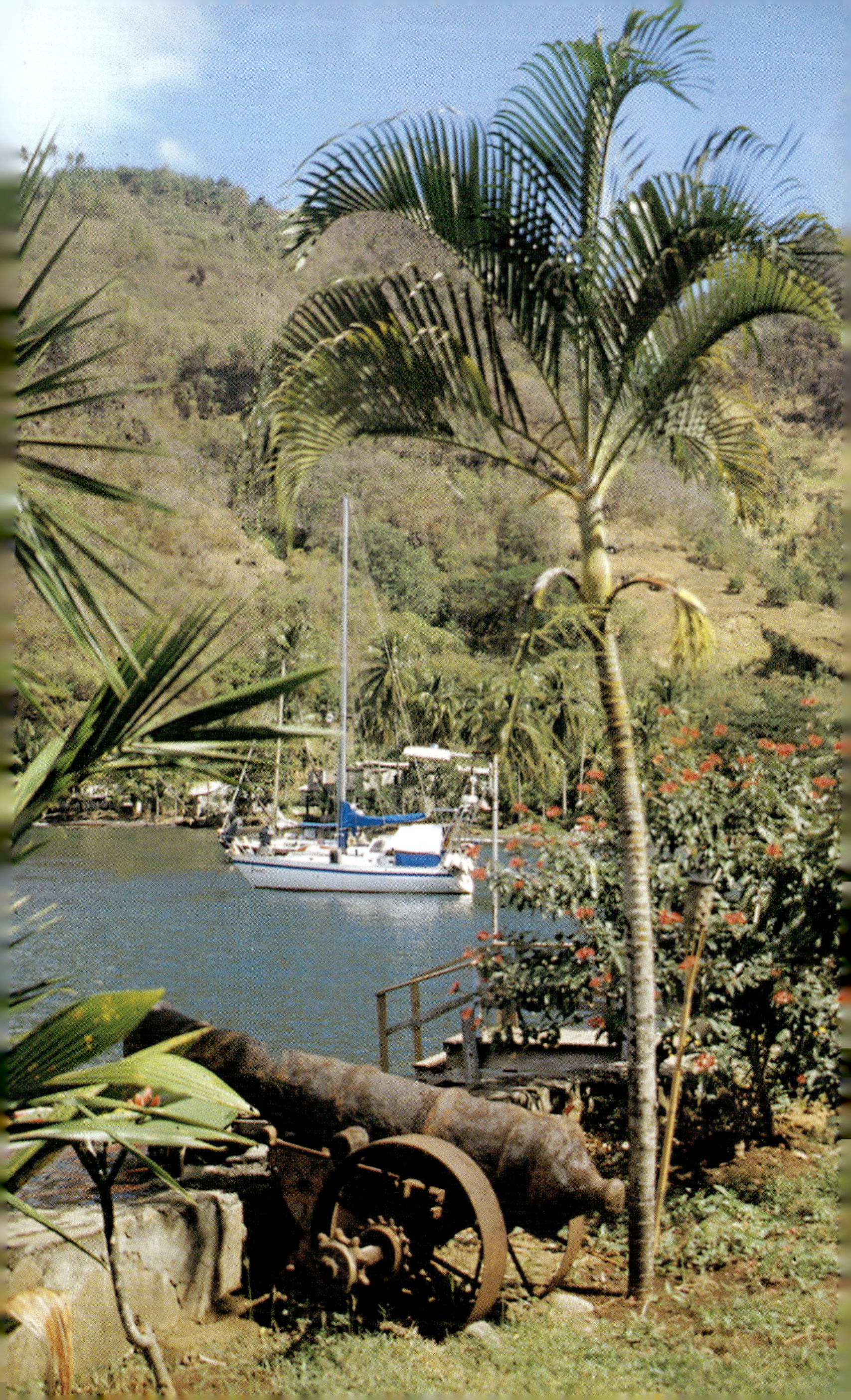

fish, is pulled in.

※ Visit the old Rutland Vale Sugar Works to see just how elaborate and ingenious the nineteenth-century engineers had to be in providing power for the sugar mills. A huge aqueduct was built to bring in water to power the massive waterwheels which in turn provided the power for the mill rollers which crushed the cane.

When the juice had been squeezed from the cane, it was boiled to produce molasses and this was then loaded in barrels on board the ships that moored just off shore.

St Vincent's most famous 𝚷 petroglyphs can be seen just past Layou, on a huge 20ft (6m) rock which is along the river bank about a quarter of a mile inland from the road. The ten-minute walk is across private land so seek permission first if not accompanied by a guide. The rock depicts many symbols including that of 'Yocahu', the Cassava God. There 𝚷 is also an important rock carving on the Calendar Stone at Mount Wynne, next to the black sand beach.

From Layou you can also detour on feeder roads inland to explore the countryside and visit the Rutland Tavern.

There were many large estates along this stretch of road, including the Peter's Hope Estate which used to process copra for oil and cassava.

This stretch of road, the Leeward Highway, is another of the island's engineering achievements, and was blasted out of the mountain sides. Before the new road was built, driving along this stretch of coastline must have been daunting because of the steep mountains, blind corners and sharp drops. Today, it offers a spectacular drive along a picturesque coastline. The highway runs from Layou to Richmond, and travels through several delightful coastal villages such as Barrouallie, Troumaca and Chateaubelair. There are also many black sand beaches en route where you can stop off and have a laze in the sun or dip in the sea provided your vehicle is safely parked off the road.

Barrouallie (pronounced Barelly), is a small fishing village with its little houses, and boats pulled up on to the beach. Fishermen here have traditionally hunted blackfish — the small pilot whale — using open boats powered by oar and using hand held harpoons.

At the school on the hill, where the children always seem to smile, there are more petroglyphs in the 𝚷

TOURING & EXPLORING ST VINCENT

school grounds. The stones are set in a lawn, and can be visited, although as you are on school property, ask permission from the school office first.

The village of Barrouallie has quite a lot of French influence, and this can be seen in the buildings and the traditional town square. The police station dates back to the 1700s and is one of the oldest buildings on the island. The cemetery is also of interest because it contains many graves of victims of the cholera epidemic which swept up the coast in 1854. Because of its strong whaling traditions, there are plans to build a whaling museum here.

Wallilabou Bay is a very popular anchorage with visiting yachts, and just inland you can visit the Wallilabou Fall where you can have a dip in the pool beneath the falls.

Chateaubelair, is the most northerly town on the west coast, and the French from Martinique are said to have built a castle here overlooking the bay although there is no trace of it. This would help explain the name which translates as either 'Castle of Beautiful Air, or 'Castle of Fair Wind'.

The road then runs on to **Richmond** where there is another Government banana reception and packing plant. You can have a swim from Richmond Beach or the nearby Wallibou Beach, while inland the landscape is dominated by Richmond Peak, with Soufriere to the north.

The road ends here but there is a path to **Trinity Falls**, so named because there are three falls, with water warmed by the many hot pools in the area. The falls, considered by many to be the most beautiful on the island, are in a deep volcanic canyon, reached by a forty-five minute walk through tropical forest, from the road. You can swim here but it is not advisable unless you are a strong swimmer as the falls and warm water combine to create swirling currents like a giant jaccuzzi. If you try to swim to the side of the pool to get out, the currents tend to spin you back in towards the centre again.

The secret of getting out of the pool is to swim towards the centre where the currents are strongest and then to let the current propel you into the shallow waters where you can get out. There are several other calm-water pools in the area if you do not fancy this one. Guides are available for the hike to the falls.

Further up the coast are the spectacular **Falls of Baleine** where the waters plunge in a

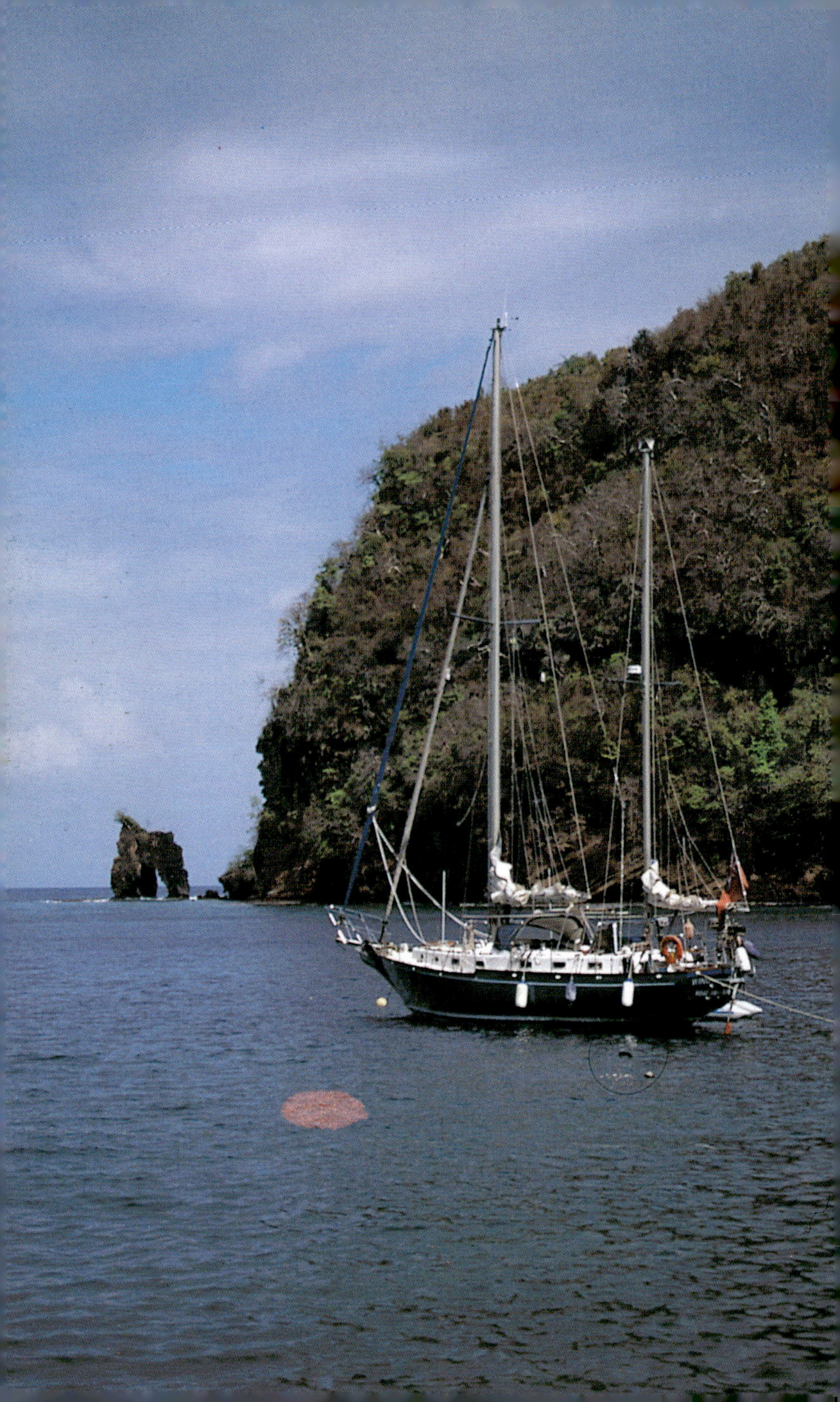

TOURING & EXPLORING ST VINCENT

Villa Beach and Young Island

opposite: Wallilabou Bay, a popular anchorage for visiting yachts

sheer drop about 60ft to the pool below. The falls can be reached after a very strenuous hike in from Fancy at the end of the Windward Highway, or from the end of the Leeward Road via the Wallibou Dry River. The best, and easiest way in, however, is to take a boat from Kingstown or one of the fishing villages up the coast, so that after landing there is only a short walk to the falls. All the area around the falls is a protected nature reserve. You can swim in the pool beneath the falls, which is surrounded by rocks over which tumble ferns and tropical foliage.

THE SOUTH COAST

Take the airport road out of Kingstown to Arnos Vale for a drive up to the summit of Dorsetshire Hill.

Dorsetshire Hill overlooks Kingstown and was the site of the last battle in the Second Carib War, during which the Carib Chieftain Chatoyer, was killed in hand-to-hand fighting. An obelisk marks the spot where he died. There are splendid views from the summit over the town, harbour, surrounding countryside and far out to sea. You reach the hill by taking Queen's Drive which starts close to the airport in Arnos Vale with its sports complex and cricket ground, and you can return down Sion Hill.

The road inland runs to Mesopotamia also known as the Marriaqua Valley (see West Coast section), while the road south continues to the magnificent **Calliaqua Bay**. Many of the island's hotels and resorts are along this stretch of coastline which has great sandy beaches and warm, safe waters to swim in. It has also become a highly fashionable residential area.

The small village of **Villa** has expanded in recent years because of the number of hotels in the area, and it stands close to Villa Beach and Indian Bay Beach, among the best on the island.

Off the shore lies **Young Island**, a private island resort offering luxurious accommodation and facilities. According to local lore, when Sir William Young was appointed Governor of St Vincent, he brought with him a large entourage including his favourite horses. One day, while entertaining, a Carib chief commented on one of the Governor's horses, and it was immediately given to him as a gift. Some time later, Sir William and the Chief were standing on the balcony of the Governor's House in Calliaqua, then the island capital, and the Governor mentioned that he thought the island off the coast was beautiful. The island was owned by the chief, and graciously, he immediately gave it Sir William as a gift.

Just beyond is **Fort Duvernette** which stands atop a towering 190ft rock. The rock is part of the Young Island estate, and used to be known as Young's Sugar Loaf because of its shape. Permission should be sought to visit the fort, although you can quite easily swim out to it. There are also usually one or two rowing boats whose owners will take you across — and collect you.

The fortress was built at the beginning of the nineteenth

century to defend Calliaqua Bay and the island's old capital, and had two gun batteries, one on the summit and one about 40ft below this. Both batteries were armed with four twenty-four pounders and an 8in mortar. One battery defended against attack from the sea, and the other from a landward attack, and the artillery pieces are still there as they were left by the departing garrison. The summit is reached by steps cut out in the rock.

Calliaqua is on the south-western corner of the island, and used to be the old capital of St Vincent. Like Marriaqua, it had its origins in a Spanish name. It was originally called *Calliagua*, meaning 'calm waters'. Over the years, however, the name changed slightly to its present form. Just beyond Calliaqua you can take the road inland for **Ribisti** to visit the old Harony Hall sugar mill. **Blue Lagoon** nestles in the corner of the island, and then you can walk around the headland overlooking **Sharp's Bay** and **Cable Hut Bay**, with Mulligan Cay just off shore.

MESOPOTAMIA & THE EAST COAST

Drive south from Kingstown and then take the Vigie Highway inland to the Marriaqua Valley, which is better known as Mesopotamia, or even 'Mespo'. Mesopotamia literally means 'Mountain Lands' and it is easy to see how it gets its name. Some of the other names, however, are slightly more obscure. La Croix was named after Madame La Croix, a French lady who owned a large estate in the valley. How the valley got its Spanish name is not clear, but there must have been a Spanish presence here at some stage because the three rivers running down the valley merge to form the Marriagua, Spanish for 'the married waters', although this name changed over the years to become Marriaqua.

Mesopotamia

This is an incredible huge fertile valley surrounded by hills on all sides, with lush vegetation everywhere. It is thought that the surrounding hills actually form the rim of a massive volcanic crater, which erupted millions of years ago. Once the pressure had been vented by the huge eruption, subterranean activity shifted northwards creating Soufriere.

The valley was not really developed until after the Second Carib War of 1795-6, because it had been a Carib stronghold until then. There was a Carib camp at

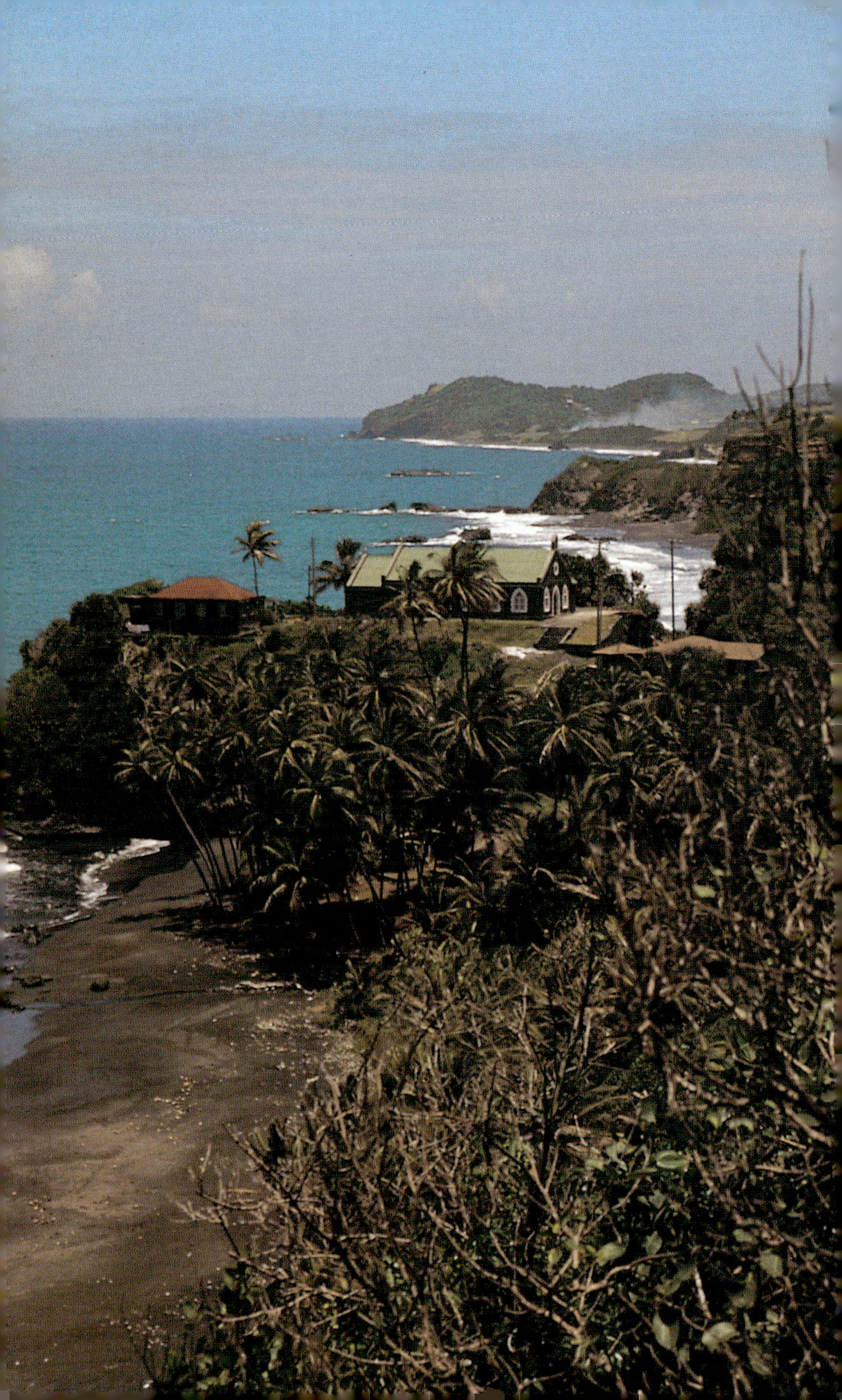

The dark-sand beaches of the east coast

opposite: Biabou, with its little Anglican church

Vigie (French for 'look out') during the Second Carib War, and it still offers commanding views over the surrounding countryside, including Kingstown. After the war, the land was sold to English settlers. It was one of the first places planted with the breadfruit brought by Captain Bligh.

The main crops are bananas, coconut, cocoa and nutmeg, but almost every other fruit and vegetables found on the island is grown here. Breadfruit is abundant, and ground crops such as eddoe, dasheen and tannia are grown in small cleared plots right up the sides of the steep valley. Most of the farms are small holdings with the farmer and his family living in small houses nestling on the sides of the valley. Terraces have been carved out on the hills for crops, and altogether there are twenty-three small agricultural villages in the valley.

Mesopotamia, with its small Roman Catholic Church, is at the mouth of the valley where the three rivers merge before running into the Yambou River, which then tumbles its way down to the eastern coast along the Yambou Gorge, which was the scene of a lot of clashes between the British and Caribs during the Carib Wars. The highest point around Mesopotamia is Grand Bonhomme, 3,181ft (970m), and the smaller peak, Petit Bonhomme, is just over 2,000ft (610m). It is likely that these French names were adapted from the original Carib word *bonum* which means 'dweller', as it is thought that the first Arawak settlers may have lived here.

Montreal is at the end of a rough road to the north west of Mesopotamia in the mountains, with magnificient views. Montreal Gardens, formerly part of a plantation around the great house, specialises in growing tropical American flowering plants commercially, especially anthuriums. There is much to see including lily ponds, wonderful exotic plants, citrus trees and a pretty stream which runs through the gardens.

You can visit the Muscovado Sugar Factory and remains of the arrowroot factories at Farm and Escape Village near the **Yambou Gorge** where there are also a number of petroglyphs to be seen.

The Mesopotamia road reaches the sea at the village of **Peruvian Vale**, and you can turn right and head south back round the coast via Argyle Beach and the Arnos Vale.

If you take this route you drive past the pretty **Argyle Beach** where there is a giant rock off shore, and an imposing church up on the hill. Argyle beach, with its crashing surf, is one of the places the islanders come to party, and cook out under the stars. Just inland up the valley is the Argyle Nature Resort, a small hotel with pool, and some of the prettiest rooms on the island.

If you turn left at the coast and head north, you come to the village of **Biabou**. The village, with its Anglican church built on the promontory, was named after a group of Caribs who landed here after fleeing from Martinique. There are the remains of a number of old arrowroot factories and sugar mills along this coastal highway. The road then runs past **Grant's Bay**, **South Union** and **North Union** to **Sans Souci**. In Union you can visit the flower centre established by Victor Hadley, which specialises in growing ginger lilies, orchids and anthuriums.

The origin of this place name, which in French means 'without care', is not known. There was a French plantation here, and it has been suggested, that the name was given because the estate was so run down.

The Windward Highway, another spectacular drive, continues to **Colonarie** with its police station. You can park in the village and explore inland on foot. Take the road inland just before the bridge past the old arrowroot factory. There is good walking in this area either following the river valley inland or along the cliffs to find your own secluded beach. The stretch of highway to Georgetown offers spectacular sea views along the way. There are also many good black sand beaches. At **Black Point** there is a man-made cavern where rum used to be stored before being rowed out into the bay where the waiting ships were anchored. Today the cavern is home to large numbers of bats.

Georgetown, named after King George III, did not really develop until the opening of the Black Point Tunnel in 1815. The 300ft (100m) long tunnel, engineered by Colonel Thomas Browne, was literally carved through the mountain which sloped steeply down into the sea. Until the tunnel, built by Carib and slave labour, was opened there was no road between the north and south of the island, and the only means of travel was by boat. The tunnel connects **Byera Bay** and **Grand Sable** and was originally used to haul sugar cane from the estates in the north of the island to the south for processing and export. After the tunnel opened, Georgetown became the sugar capital of the island, and the Mount Bentick factory, which finally closed in 1984, was the last operating sugar plant on the island. Today, the town is a shadow of its former self, but is useful as the starting point for exploration further north and inland. It has a pleasant main street with its overhanging balconies, churches and small library.

After Georgetown, the road deteriorates the further north one drives, and if you are heading for Fancy, the journey is best continued in a four-wheel-drive vehicle. If you have driven from Kingstown, you can park in Georgetown and take a four-wheel drive taxi further north. If you only want to reach the Sandy Bay area, however, the journey can be undertaken in an ordinary car, although care needs to be taken, especially after wet weather.

Shortly after Georgetown you have to cross the huge Rabacca Dry River, formed by the flow of volcanic ash from Soufriere during the 1902 eruption. The river now drains both the eastern slopes of Soufriere and nearby Mount Brisbane. Because the volcanic earth is porous, the river suddenly disappears underground about a mile upstream.

For most of the year, the dry river, which is several hundred feet across, looks more like a huge gravel pit through which the road snakes, but after heavy rain it becomes a raging torrent and crossings should not be attempted. At least two lorries and a tractor have been swept into the sea by the fast flowing waters. Hopefully the shack that has been built half-way across the river bed is sufficiently high above the ground to escape the flood waters. Gravel from the river bed is taken south by road to a plant where it is mixed with cement to produce building blocks.

Rabacca Farms used to be known as Orange Hill Estate and ran from near the coast to the slopes of Soufriere , making it one of the world's largest coconut estates, extending to almost 3,200 acres. It has now been divided into a number of small farms as part of the Government's Rural Development Project, but still produces bananas, coconuts, citrus and spices, as well as aubergines and cola nuts, used for flavouring what must now be the world's most popular carbonated drink. You can see arrowroot growing by the roadside, and there are ruins of several sugar and arrowroot mills, plus the elaborate structures including aqueducts, which used to carry the water in to power the machinery.

The best way of getting to **Soufriere** is from a track which starts in the banana and coconut plantations of Rabacca Farms. There is a huge sign for the trail by the road and you take the turning to the left to drive to the trail head. You can hike around the rim of the huge volcano, more than a mile across, and then either return to the east coast, or make your way down to the western coast. The hike to the west coast follows a gully carved out by lava flowing from Soufriere into the Caribbean, and you can hit the coast at either Richmond Vale or further south at Chateaubelair. It is advisable to have a guide for this trip, and if you plan to cross the island, make sure that arrangements are made

TOURING & EXPLORING ST VINCENT

SOUFRIERE — ST VINCENT'S ACTIVE VOLCANO

Soufriere, because of its frequent eruptions, is one of the most studied volcanoes in the world and it attracts vulcanologists from around the world. There were major eruptions in 1718 and 1812, when the cloud of volcanic ash blocked out the sun as far away as Barbados. The huge crater was formed after the 1902 eruption, and the last eruption was on Good Friday, 13 April 1979, although the many vents and bubbling hot pools show that there is still a lot of subterranean activity. The summit is often cloaked in clouds, but on fine days the views from the top across to both the east and west coasts, are breathtaking.

A large sign indicates the way to the Soufriere trail

for a car or boat to pick you up, as it is a long way back into Kingstown.

The trail is quite steep and steadily climbs volcanic ridges for just under 3½ miles (5.2km) until you reach Soufriere 4,048ft (1,234m) above sea level. It is almost 1,500ft (460m) down onto the floor of the crater. The landscape is quite startling and stark in comparison with the lush, tropical vegetation to be found further south and encountered on the walk in.

The walk starts through lush tropical vegetation, with exotic flowers and towering bamboo. It then climbs through tropical rain forest and long trousers are advised, and then the trail emerges on to the grassy uplands, scored by deep lava gorged canyons, the first signs of volcanic activity.

The final ascent to the rim of the crater is steep and over volcanic debris and brittle lava, where only a few lichens and mosses are able to survive. There are sulphur vents on the southern rim, and there are trails down into the crater, but remember, it is a steep climb back out.

After walking round the volcano you can either return by the same way, making a round trip of about 7½ miles (12km), or you can carry on to the west coast. If you choose the western route it is a good 10 miles (16km) to the coast, which means the whole trip is about 15 miles (24km) altogether, a good day's walking in view of the heat, ascent and terrain.

Back on the Windward Highway, the road runs into **Sandy Bay**, where native Caribs were settled after the Carib Wars, and then it is a short drive to **Owia**, another Carib village on the north-eastern tip of the island. It is noted for the arrowroot processing mill and the salt ponds, both of which can be visited.

Arrowroot is a member of the Maranta family, whose roots and rhizomes produce an edible starch. While there are many species of arrowroot, the best is *Marant arundinacea*, better known as West Indies arrowroot. The plant grows to about 6ft (1.8m) tall and throws out fleshy tuberous roots, which are really underground storage systems.

The plant's life cycle includes spells of rapid growth and then dormancy, and the starch stored in the roots allows it to survive these dormant periods. The crop is harvested just before the plant goes into a dormant stage. The roots are peeled, grated in water, and the mixture then dried to a powder which is purified by repeated rinses.

Arrowroot is one of the purest known forms of edible starch, and is easily digested, so has been traditionally used in baby foods, as well as in cooking for thickening sauces, soups and puddings. St Vincent has traditionally been one of the world's major suppliers of arrowroot, and the discovery that arrowroot improved the quality and traction of computer print out paper, gave the industry a massive boost.

The Owia Salt Ponds make a natural swimming pool by the sea because of a series of volcanic ridges just off the coast. Swimming along this stretch of coastline is not normally advisable because of the powerful waves and onshore winds, but at Owia, the series of offshore ridges have the effect of reducing the power of the waves, so that by the time they reach the rock pools the water is calm and safe for swimming. There is also an impressive series of steps down the cliff to the water. From the cliffs you can usually see St Lucia, about 20 miles (32km) to the north west.

After **Commantawana Bay**, you reach the tiny village of **Fancy**, another Carib village, and the end of the road. There is a trail which starts here and travels west around the coast to the Falls of Baleine but it is a very strenuous hike. It is not advisable unless you are a very fit, experienced walker and a guide is essential. The best way to see these falls is by boat as described on the west coast route.

overleaf: Near Black Point Bay

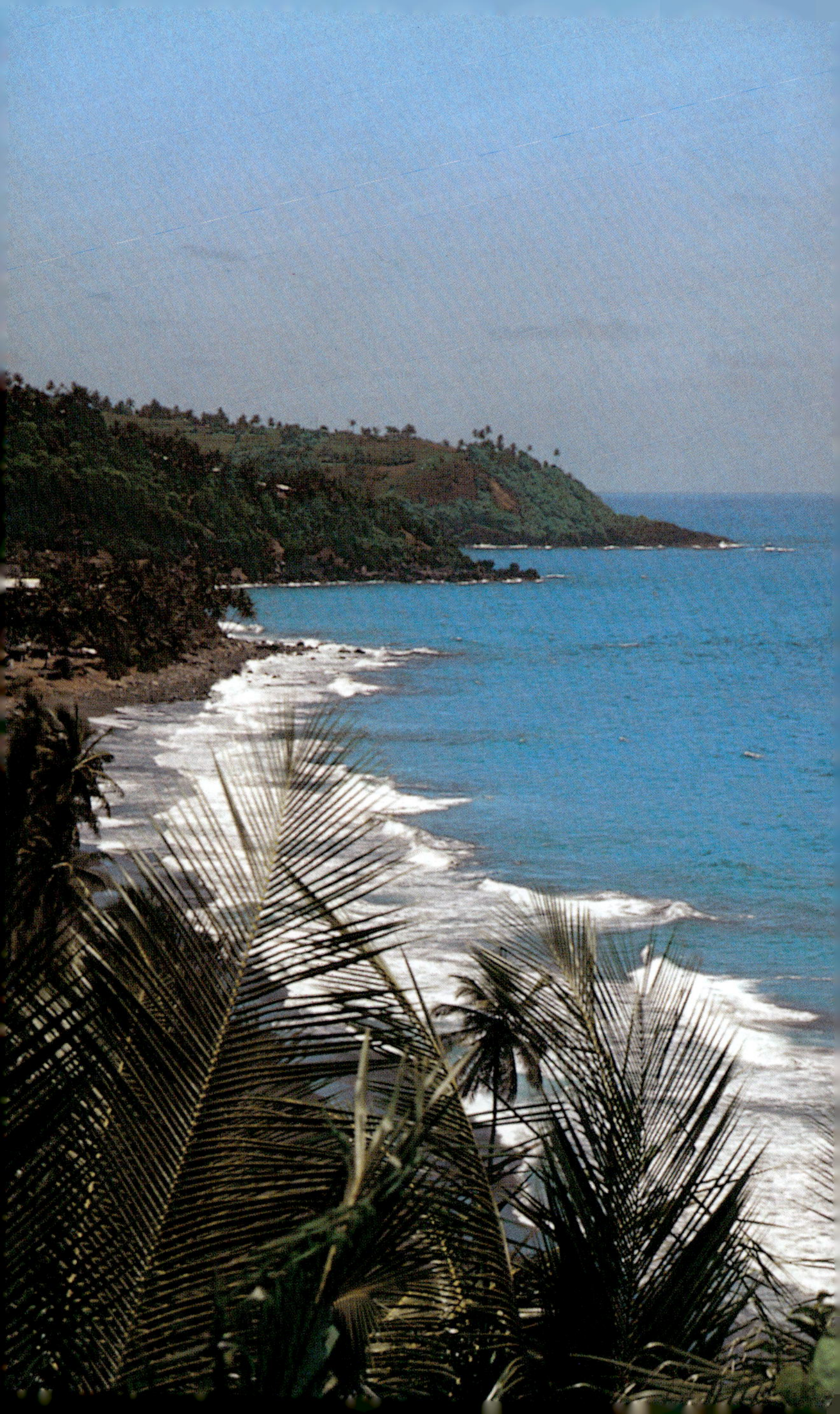

EATING OUT

$ = inexpensive
$$ = moderate
$$$ = expensive

In & Around Kingstown

Aggie's Restaurant and Bar
Grenville Street
Kingstown
☎ 456-2110
Excellent West Indian and seafood $-$$

Amor's Restaurant and Bar
Stoney Ground
Kingstown
☎ 457-9829
Healthy cuisine $-$$

The Attic
Corner of Melville and Grenville Streets
Kingstown
☎ 457-2558
West Indian and Continental $-$$. Live music and nightly entertainment. Fun place.

Basil's Bar & Restaurant
Bay Street
Kingstown
☎ 457-2713
International $-$$

Bella Vista Inn
Kingstown Park
☎ 457-2757
Creole $-$$

Bounty Restaurant
Halifax Street
Kingstown
☎ 456-1776
Fast food and local specialities $-$$

Chung Wa Restaurant & Bar
Bay Street
Kingstown
☎ 457-2566
Chinese $-$$

Cobblestone Roof Top Restaurant
Bay Street
Kingstown
☎ 456-1937
Fast Food and West Indian specialities for breakfast and lunch $-$$

D-Tunnel
Overlooking Camden Park Industrial Centre
☎ 457-8606
West Indian/International. Nightly entertainment $-$$

Horseshoe Restaurant and Bar
Grenville Street
Kingstown
☎ 457-2042
West Indian specialities $-$$

Joyce's Snackette
Bay Street
Kingstown
☎ 456-2823
West Indian fastfood and specialities $

Kentucky Fried Chicken
Grenville Street
Kingstown
☎ 457-2612
Fast food $

Le Café
Halifax Street
☎ 457-2791
International $-$$

Moore's Delight
Corner of Middle and Egmont Streets
☎ 456-1928
West Indian specialities $

Nice Foods Unlimited
Heron Hotel complex
Kingstown
☎ 456-1391
West Indian and international $-$$

Sid's Pub
Grenville Street
Kingstown
☎ 456-2315
Excellent West Indian and Creole Specialities $-$$. Sports pub and lively place.

Vee Jay's Restaurant and Bar
Bay Street
Kingstown
☎ 457-2845

On the West Coast

Emerald Valley Casino
Penniston Valley
☎ 456-7140
Light meals and drinks are served in the casino $-$$.
The pool-side restaurant offers West Indian and international dishes $$.

Stephen's Hideout
Cumberland Bay
☎ 458-2325
Seafood and West Indian specialities $-$$

Wallilabou Anchorage
Wallilabou Bay
☎ 458-7270
West Indian specialities $-$$

In the South

A La Mer Restaurant
Indian Bay Beach
☎ 458-4001
West Indian and International $-$$

Argyle Nature Resort
Overlooking Argyle Beach
☎ 458-0992
International and seafood specialities $-$$

Beachcombers
Villa Beach
☎ 458-4283
West Indian and International $-$$

Chicken Roost
Arnos Vale
☎ 456-4932
Fast food $

The Coral Room
Sunset Shores
Villa Beach
☎ 458-4411
West Indian and seafood $-$$

Dolphins Villa
☎ 457-4337
Specialises in seafood, Creole and continental cuisine $-$$

French Restaurant
Villa Beach
☎ 458-4972
French and seafood $-$$

Grand View Restaurant
Villa Point
☎ 458-4811
West Indian and International $-$$

Lagoon Hotel and Marina
Blue Lagoon
☎ 458-4308
International and seafood $$

Lime 'N' Pub
Villa Beach
☎ 458-4227
West Indian $-$$

Pizza Party
Arnos Vale
☎ 456-4932
Pizza $

Villa Lodge
Villa Lodge Hotel
Villa Point
☎ 458-4641
Seafood and West Indian specialities $-$$

Young Island Resort
Young Island
☎ 458-4826
Seafood and continental $$-$$$

On the East Coast

Ferdie's Restaurant and Bar
Georgetown
☎ 458-6433
West Indian specialities $-$$

THE GRENADINES

- Bequia
- Petit Nevis
- Battow
- Isle à Quatre
- Baliceau
- Mustique
- Petit Mustique
- Petit Canouan
- Canouan
- Mayreau
- Union Island
- Tobago Cays
- Palm Island
- Petit St Vincent

Touring & Exploring The Grenadines

BEQUIA

Bequia is the largest of the St Vincent Grenadines and covers about seven square miles. It was known by the Caribs as Becouya — the 'Island of the Cloud', although no-one knows why, because although the island is hilly, the tallest point is only 881ft (268m) above sea level and rarely cloaked in cloud. Perhaps the Caribs arrived on one of the few days when it was raining.

Bequia, pronouced 'Beck-way', can be reached by boat and air,

A small quayside market at Port Elizabeth harbour, Bequia

and although only 9 miles (14.5km) from Kingstown, the crossing can sometimes be a little rough. But if the crossing to Bequia is smooth then there will be plenty of time to enjoy the views in the sunshine as the boat sails out of Kingstown and then approaches Bequia, travelling down the west coast of the island to Port Elizabeth. Unfortunately the return journey may be rougher. The trouble is that if the seas are running a little rough, you do not realise it all the time you are in the lee of the island. It is only when you pass Bequia Head at the northern tip of the island that you are suddenly hit by the winds and waves, and then it is rock and roll all the way back to Kingstown. This is not meant to put you off, because the island is definitely worth visiting and staying on, but if you are a bad sailor, fly in, or wait for calm seas! A good way of gauging the island's popularity is that many St Vincentians choose to holiday there every year.

Work on Bequia Airport started in April, 1990 and the 3,200ft (975m) runway was completed in 1992, making the island accessible by air for the first time. The airport is on the south coast and serviced by LIAT, Mustique Airways, SVG Air and Air Carriacou.

The island has had a very troubled past because of its strategic location, and the French and British fought over it for almost 200 years during the seventeenth and eighteenth centuries. At that time there were also legends that the island was fabulously wealthy with gold and diamonds to be picked up, but the only gold was the golden sands.

In 1664 France claimed possession of all the Grenadines, largely because the many natural harbours that provided shelter for her fleet, and also because the forested islands, provided timber for building and repairing the ships. There was no attempt to settle the island, however, and the first people to arrive from across the Atlantic, were shipwrecked slaves who made it ashore in 1675 after their vessel foundered. Many of the survivors stayed on Bequia and some married the Caribs already living there. The descendants of these marriages are known as Black-Caribs.

Bequia became part of St Vincent under a treaty worked out in 1762, and the following year with the Treaty of Paris, St Vincent and the Grenadines were ceded to Britain. The French retook the islands in 1779 but they were finally restored to Britain four years later by the Treaty of Versailles.

Among the first English settlers were the Warners, and their plantation at Spring became so successful that others came to the island to grow sugar cane using slave labour. After emancipation, however, this sort of estate was no longer economic, many of the population left the island, and the land was divided into many smaller farms. Around this time the Wallace family arrived from Scotland, and in 1830 Sir William Wallace managed the Friendship Estate, and one of his sons, Bill, founded the whaling industry with Frenchman Joseph Ollivierre, who had bought the Paget Farm Estate.

Bequia is still one of the few places in the world where whaling is legal, although there is only one open boat still engaged in this, an 18ft wooden boat built on the island, which used to be rowed but now has a sail. A replacement sail boat was being built by hand the last time I visited the island.

There is also a small whaling museum in the Paget Farm home of Athneal Ollivierre, known as the 'Last Harpooner', and grandson of Joseph. The entrance from the road to the white and blue painted house is under a pair of huge whale bones.

For many years whaling ships from New England, were based on the island. Today, when whales are sighted, the boat puts out to sea, and its crew are often guided to the hunting area by the crowds standing on Mount Pleasant. If a whale is killed, and this is becoming an increasingly rare occurrence, it is towed into shallow waters for processing. While whaling has largely been banned, it has been a tradition on Bequia for many centuries, and this is why a special dispensation was granted to the islanders by the International Whaling Commission to catch up to three whales a year, usually between February and April. On average one whale a year is killed and it is a time of great celebration on the island. There are the remains of a whaling station on Petit Nevis that can be visited. At the height of the whaling industry, there were six whaling stations on or around the island. All commercial whaling ended in 1920.

State Prime Minister James Mitchell is from Bequia, and despite his many official duties, he still finds time to return to his family home on the island.

Bequia has a population of 4,868, and life has not changed much over the years although there are now a few more tourists around. Fishing is still the main

SHOPPING ON BEQUIA

Bequia is noted for its boutiques, studios and crafts shops. Gift ideas include local hand-painted articles and wall coverings, jewellery, and the famous Bequia hand-made model boats, on sale at Mauvin's Model Boat Shop and Sargeant Brothers Model Boat Shop, both in Port Elizabeth and just past the covered market. The Crab Hole boutique, set in its wonderful gardens, offers equally wonderful clothes, hand silk-screened and sewn. You can watch the silk-screening process, and even have your own design printed. It also has a wide range of other gifts and souvenirs. Rastafashion on Friendship Bay produces hand-painted T-shirts, as well as local crafts and island jewellery.

Shops on Bequia are open between 8am and noon, or 9am and 1pm, and again between 2pm and 6pm. The three banks, Barclays, Caribbean Banking Corporation and National Commercial Bank, all in Port Elizabeth, are open Monday to Thursday 8am to 1pm, and on Friday from 8am to 1pm and 3pm to 5pm. The Post Office is open Monday to Friday from 9am to noon and 1pm to 3pm, and on Saturday between 9am and 11.30am.

opposite: The golden sands of Admiralty Bay, Bequia

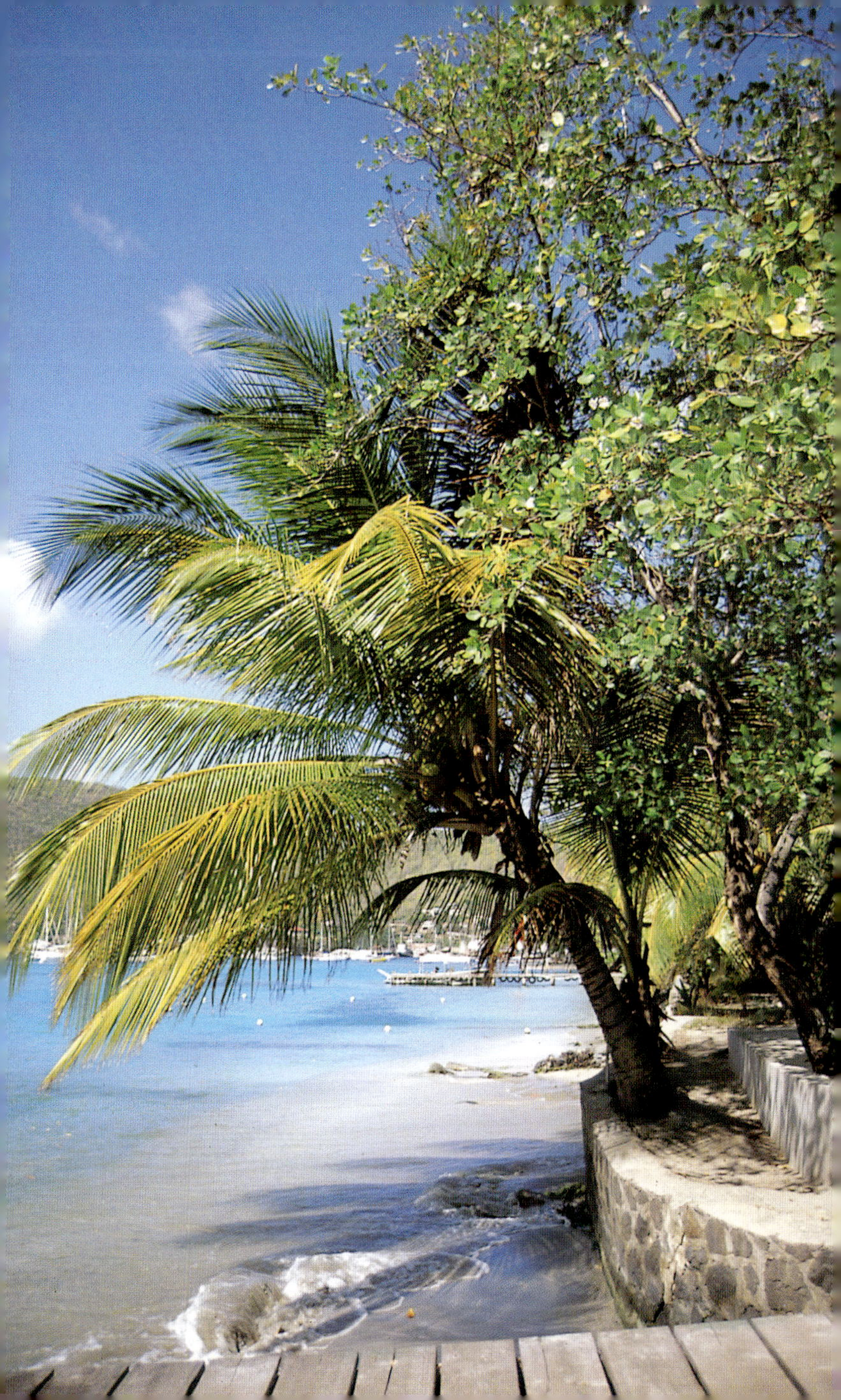

occupation and a new fish processing plant has been built on the south coast.

The islanders are also skilled seamen, and many serve with the merchant marine and others skipper and crew the cruise yachts based on Bequia.

Bequia also has a long tradition of skilled boatbuilding, and many of the original shipwrights were of Scottish origin. Many of the boats, sloops and schooners built on Bequia, still ply the islands.

Ferries arrive at the jetty in Port Elizabeth which lies in the great sweep of **Admiralty Bay**. As the ferry rounds the headland to enter the bay it passes the battery, built in the late eighteenth century on the cliffs at Hamilton, and it also has to negotiate the reefs offshore, notably the Devil's Table Reef.

Close to the jetty is the tourist information office, with the police and customs station just to the left. Taxi drivers will descend on you in droves offering lifts to your destination. While it looks chaotic, there is a sort of order, and you should take the taxi at the head of the queue. Expect to pay around US$15 an hour if you want to hire a taxi to take you sightseeing or to one of the beaches.

Water taxis are also available and boats with a number on the front are accredited by the Bequia Tourist Office, but most do not carry insurance or enough life rafts and the like, so be warned.

Anchorage Bay is a large sheltered natural harbour which has attracted yachts from around the world for many years. The Bequia Yacht Marina was re-opened in 1993 and every year it services yachts from around the world, and while repairs are being carried out, the sailors can relax in the Harpoon Saloon, which overlooks the harbour.

The small **Port Elizabeth** waterfront is usually busy and packed when the ferry is docked. At night, it is very picturesque with several small bars and restaurants and the lights of the anchored yachts bobbing out in the bay.

Admiralty Bay is divided into a number of beaches, including **Princess Margaret Beach** because she bathed here in 1958 — and **Lower Bay**, a two mile walk from Port Elizabeth, with a small fishing village.

Palm-fringed **Friendship Bay** is due south of Port Elizabeth on the southern coast, and is the longest beach on the island. Offshore you can spot Petit Nevis, where there is a whaling station, and Ile de Quatre. **Hope Bay** lies to the east on the Atlantic Ocean side. Port Elizabeth was named in 1937 to commemorate the coronation of the present queen's parents.

The islanders say that there are enough roads to get to where you need to go, which is not strictly true but Bequia was made for exploring on foot, and there are many delightful hikes, none of them very taxing, although inland it is quite hilly. Roads run across the island to Hope Bay, where there is a working coconut plantation, and up the eastern coast as far as Spring, where there are a number of sugar mill ruins just beyond the Spring Bay Hotel and further north at Brute Point. There is a lovely walk from Port Elizabeth to **Spring Bay** where there is a 200-year-old working plantation and delightful small hotel, overlooking the ocean, and you can cool down with a swim before heading back. The restaurant largely uses produce grown on the estate or caught just offshore. The old sugar mill was working until 1905. You can also continue on to Industry, about a mile further on, where there are trails to Bequia Head and across the island to Anse Chein on the north west coast.

The roads also run south along Admiralty Bay to Lower Bay, and to the Friendship Bay area and then along the south coast for a little way. Former British Prime Minister Sir Anthony Eden used to own a property on Friendship Bay.

There is also a road up to **Mount Pleasant**, one of the best vantage points on the island.

The Bequia Casualty Hospital is in Port Elizabeth ☎ 458-3294, and there are five churches on the island, representing the Anglican, Roman Catholic, Evangelical, Seventh Day Adventists and Jehovah's Witness faiths.

The St Mary's Anglican church in Port Elizabeth, dates back to 1829 and it is worth spending some time reading the fascinating memorial tablets. It is built of local limestone and bricks imported as ships' ballast, and replaced the first church blown down in 1798.

There is accommodation to suit all tastes from the excellent Plantation House with its fine restaurant — one of the Caribbean's rising gastronomic stars, to small, comfortable guest houses. The food is good and the Bequians like to party, so there are often dances and jump ups, as well as the more organised events such as hotel beach barbecues and so on.

And, if you are staying on Bequia, take the time to visit St Vincent and some of the other Grenadines. There are lots of day trips available to visit the other

Friendship Bay, Bequia

opposite: *Spring Bay, Bequia*

BEACHES & WATERSPORTS ON BEQUIA

Bequia's fabulous beaches are often secluded, and always sandy, The island also offers great diving. There are thirty-five major dive sites around the island, none more than 15 minutes away by boat, although there is no shore diving. You can even visit the wreck of the MS *Lireco*, a 110ft freighter, that was specially sunk in 1986 as a facility for divers. A dive to the wreck also allows you to see how quickly the vessel has been colonised by all sorts of marine life, including coral and sponges.

Watersports are available from Dive Bequia at Plantation House, Sunsports at the Gingerbread complex, Dive Paradise at the Friendship Bay Hotel, and Bequia Dive at Friendship Bay.

De Reef Aquasports in Lower Bay and Paradise Windsurfing in Friendship also offer windsurfing. There is a restaurant and beach bar.

islands, including mini-cruises on the *Friendship Rose*, the magnificent 80ft schooner, which for 25 years served as the mail boat between the islands. It was taken out of service in 1992 and now, after an extensive refit, she carries passengers on day trips between St Vincent and Bequia and Mustique or the Tobago Cays.

CANOUAN

The island is named after the Carib word for 'turtle', because so many of these sea creatures came ashore to lay eggs on its many sandy beaches. It has also been suggesed that the island gets its name because it is shaped like a turtle, but that requires a great deal of imagination — or several glasses of rum.

Today, these beaches, which claim to be among the best in the Caribbean, play host to holidaymakers who really want to get away from it all. The island is small, only three and a half miles by one and a quarter, and has a population about 740. Inland there are gently rolling hills where you can stroll without seeing anyone else, except perhaps a young boy looking after the family's small herd of goats. There used to be a large gun mounted on the summit of the hill known as Fort Caribe. The old stone Anglican Church, which dates from the early nineteenth century, sits on a hill in the north of the island, looking out to sea. The church and the village surrounding it were badly damaged by a hurricane in 1921 and abandoned, as the people relocated to Charlestown in the south.

There is an airport towards the southern tip of the island which has night landing facilities, and Air Martinique run scheduled flights from St Vincent. Mustique Airways and SVG Air also provide charter services. If you are planning to fly in to Canouan, however, do it during the daytime if possible, because the views of the area as you fly over the islands is one you will not forget. You can sail your own vessel to the island, or catch the MV *Snapper*, which leaves Kingstown on Mondays, Thursdays and Saturdays at 10.30am and arrives in Canouan about four and a half hours later.

The Canouan Beach Hotel has guest cottages overlooking the golden sands and gently breaking surf, and offers sailing, snorkelling and day cruises to the other islands. Expansion plans include a marina, small shopping complex and more guest facilities.

The Tamarind Beach Hotel and

Yacht Club is a new luxury all-inclusive resort with forty-eight lovely guest rooms and fine dining, offering Italian, Creole and Continental cuisines. There are facilities for a wide range of watersports and cruises.

The Anchor Inn has four comfortable rooms. The Crystal Apartments Restauant and Bar is also on the beach with two apartments and a small restaurant and bar, while Villa Le Bijou, a small and very good value guest house, sits on top of the hill, offering spectacular views all round, and six rooms.

MUSTIQUE

This gem of an island is often in the headlines because of the rich and famous who regularly drop in, most notably Princess Margaret. Raquel Welch. Mick Jagger and David Bowie all own villas on the island.

Named by the French after the mosquito swarms first found there, the island is now one of the most exclusive resorts in the world. The small island, just three miles by one and a half miles, covering about 3,500 acres, with 12 miles (19km) of coastline and safe beaches, has a population of about 650, and is privately-owned. It has been beautifully developed by Colin Tennant, whose aim was to establish it as an international community. He bought the island in 1959, and it is now run by the Mustique Company which represents the island property owners. It is an island of green, gently sloping hills surrounded on all sides by white sandy beaches and turquoise seas, making it an ideal tropical hideaway.

There is great snorkelling along the west coast at **Endeavour**, **Plantation**, **Britannia** and **Lagoon Bays**, and water skiing in Britannia Bay. The island is ten minutes' flying time from St Vincent, six hours from New York and ten hours from London. By sea it is about two and a half miles from Kingstown, and the Mustique Company boat can provide transportation to neighbouring islands.

The annual average temperature is between 75°F and 85°F (24-29°C), and the island gets between 45 and 60 inches (112-150cm) of rain a year, most of which falls between late-August and mid-November.

The island is quite hilly and really consists of seven valleys, each running down to its own sandy beach, with a plain in the north. Inland the wooded valleys

The luxurious Cotton House is Mustique's only hotel

TOURING & EXPLORING THE GRENADINES

rise to around 500ft (150m). Offshore there are many coral reefs, protecting the twelve miles of coastline. Britannia Bay on the south coast and Macaroni Bay on the north coast are among the island's best beaches.

The island, although owned by the Mustique Company, is part of the state of St Vincent and the Grenadines, and the Prime Minister sits on the board.

The airstrip is in the north of the island with a nature reserve between it and Cotton House. The island's cricket pitch is between the nature reserve and Endeavour Bay, and south of the airstrip is the island's church and fully-equipped doctor's clinic. The stables for horse riding are to the east of the airstrip. Riding is mostly early in the day or late in the afternoon when the temperatures are not too high for both riders and horses.

Most of the islanders live in **Lovell Village** close to the headland between Plantain and Britannia Bays.

The wreck of the 20,000 ton French liner, the *Antilles*, lies off

Mustique is a tropical paradise

l'Ansecoy Bay on the northern coast. It is possible to take a day charter to Mustique, and then you can walk round the island in a couple of hours and rub shoulders with the rich. You can even rent a scooter and be really lazy.

While villas are expensive to rent, they are affordable if a group of friends or family get together to share the cost.

The only hotel on the island is the sumptious Cotton House, a spacious eighteenth-century great house, which has been superbly adapted for its present use. The house was built in stone and coral and many of the public rooms retain their original character with antique furnishings, and the bedrooms are exquisite. The elegant restaurant offers international cuisine, and afternoon tea has become a firm tradition to the accompaniment of classical music. The hotel set in 13 acres, has its own tennis courts and horse riding stable.

There are a number of villas on the island which are available for rent through the Mustique Company. As most of the villas are owned by the famous and very wealthy, this is reflected in both the luxury standard of accommodation offered which usually comes with maid and cook, and the rental charges asked for it.

Firefly House is a private house overlooking Britannia Bay and it offers rooms with breakfast for those want to enjoy the Mustique life style at very reasonable cost. It was the first house built on the island.

Balliceaux and **Battowia** are two small islands off Mustique. Balliceaux, a corruption of the French *belles oiseaux* meaning 'beautiful birds', was the island the Caribs were sent to in 1797 after the Carib War, prior to their transportation to Honduras.

MAYREAU

Mayreau is a small, privately-owned island covering about one square mile, with a population of about 180, and reached only by boat. It is a 30-minute trip from Union Island, and even the mail boat has to be met in the bay by smaller craft which take on board supplies for the island. The larger cruise ships also disgorge their passengers into smaller boats to be ferried ashore. It has several white sand beaches, one resort hotel on the sweeping Salt Whistle Bay. There are no roads, and electricity is provided by generators.

TOBAGO CAYS

The Tobago Cays are south of Canouan and east of Mayreau, and offer world-class diving. The Cays largely consist of five small islands — Petit Rameau, Petit Bateau, Jamesby, Baradal and Petit Tobac. The islands are noted for their serrated coastlines which create hundreds of tiny coves, bays and inlets to explore and enjoy. The islands are also protected by a ring of coral reefs — World's End Reef and Horseshoe Reef — and can only be reached by boat, so you really can enjoy the luxury of your own near-deserted tropical island.

PALM ISLAND

Another tiny, beautiful privately owned island with a resort featuring twenty-four stone cottages all facing on to the beautiful white sands of Casuarina Beach. There is an open air restaurant and all manner of watersports are available. The island really does boast some of the most beautiful beaches in the Caribbean, if not the world, such as Coral Bay, Tamarind Beach, Coral Cove and Secret Beach.

The island used to be called Prune Island, although no-one knows why, and the name was changed when it was acquired on lease in 1966 by John and Mary Caldwell, who achieved fame by sailing around the world in *Outward Bound*, a yacht they built themselves. They planted hundred, if not thousands, of palm trees on Palm Island and the other Grenadines, and single-handedly eradicated every mosquito on the island. Snorkelling safaris are offered and there is even a jogging trail! Access by air is via the airport on Union Island and then boat for the one-mile crossing.

PETIT ST VINCENT

This island, often referred to as simply PSV, is the most southerly of the Grenadines which comes under the jurisdiction of St Vincent. It used to be owned by Lilly Bethel, who came from Petit Martinique, and her sons ran a fleet of trading schooners among the islands. In the 1960s, she was persuaded to sell to an American consortium, who developed the present resort, which is popular with visiting yachts.

The tiny island is now one large 113-acre luxury resort with rolling hills and woodland, surrounded by stunning white beaches, and reefs offshore. Guest cottages are widely spaced for privacy among lush scenery, each with their own private patio and magnificent views. Breakfast and room service is delivered 'meals on wheels' style by staff driving the hotel's customised vehicles. There is a restaurant and bar, boutique, tennis and boats for charters and trips.

UNION ISLAND

Union Island covers 2,070 acres, about 3.2 square miles (8.4 sq km), and has a population of about 1,930. It is remarkably hilly and approaching the island by sea from the south, there appear to be three sets of hills — in the east, in the centre of the island

Palm Island — the perfect hideaway

opposite: There is a warm welcome at Union Island's small airport

TOURING & EXPLORING THE GRENADINES

and in the west. The most spectacular is the towering central hill known as The Pinnacle which rises to more than 900ft (274m) above sea level. The sides are so steep that it has often been described as looking like the spire of a cathedral.

On the western side of the island there are a series of three hills: Mount Parnassus, Mount Tabor and Mount Olympus which run south to north, and Fort Hill, named because of the fort which used to protect the harbour and sea approaches, dominates the eastern side of Union Island. The approach by boat from tobago Cays is even more spectacular.

The MV *Snapper* calls at Union Island on Mondays, Thursdays and Saturdays. The airport has regular scheduled services from LIAT and Air Martinique, and Mustique Airways and SVG Air offer charter services. It is a busy little airport because apart from bringing in passengers planning to stay on Union Island, it also ferries in many others who are catching boat connections to neighbouring islands, or going cruising.

The island boasts fabulous beaches and is a favourite watering hole for yachts on passage through the Grenadines and Eastern Caribbean. **Clifton** is the main town and port, and the waterfront has a number of charming small inns. It is joined with Ashton, the island's other small town by a coast road which offers stunning views out to sea over the coral shelf towards Carriacou.

Union Island has a busy harbour and is the Port of Entry for the southern Grenadines. The island makes a good base if you are planning a sailing holiday around the neighbouring islands.

The airport is just north of Clifton on the eastern edge of the island. The small tourist information bureau is to the left when you get off the ferry, and the Post Office and Anchorage Hotel to the right. The small clinic is along the bay south of the tourist office.

The Anchorage Yacht Club is between the airstrip and the sea, and is able to accommodate guests who want to fly or sail in. The club offers rooms or bungalows on the water's edge, and the restaurant Les Pieds dans l'Eau, is noted for its excellent breakfasts, and tempting Creole and French cuisine. It makes a great centre for sailing, diving, watersports or just flopping on the beach, and watching everyone else. At night there are often steel bands and jump-ups.

The Clifton Beach Hotel also offers accommodation, and in

addition, has a number of cottages and apartments at different locations around the island. The hotel's waterfront restaurant is well-known for its local specialities.

The Sunny Grenadines is also on the waterfront in lush tropical gardens, and many of the rooms overlook the harbour. The hotel is also a yacht charter centre.

The island boasts several fine and safe beaches with excellent scuba and snorkelling offshore. Dive Anchorage offers diving tuition and trips, and can arrange a variety of other watersports.

EATING OUT ON THE GRENADINES

$ = inexpensive
$$ = moderate
$$$ = expensive

Bequia

Cafe King Fisher
☎ 458-3575
Snacks and specialities $

Coco's Place
Lower Bay
☎ 458-3463.
Local specialities. Good value and meals served all day $

Cool Spot Restaurant and Bar
Back Street
Port Elizabeth
☎ 458-3586
West Indian and seafood $-$$

Crescent Inn Beach Bar
Industry Beach
☎ 458-3400
Seafood and West Indian specialities. $-$$ Barbecues are held every full moon!

Daphne's
Port Elizabeth
☎ 458-3271
West Indian specialities and seafood $-$$

Dawn's Creole
Lower Bay
☎ 458-3154
Creole specialities and seafood $-$$

De Reef
Lower Bay
☎ 457-3104
West Indian cuisine $-$$

El Mirador
Hamilton
☎ 457-3080
Seafood and Spanish foods and wine $-$$

Flame Tree Restaurant
Blue Tropic Hotel
Friendship Bay
☎ 458-3573
Local cuisine and steaks a speciality
$$

Frangipani Hotel Restaurant
Admiralty Bay
☎ 458-3255.
West Indian and International
$-$$$

Gingerbread Cafe
Admiralty Bay
☎ 458-3800
Snacks and delicious home baked cakes. Daily lunch BBQ. $

Gingerbread Restaurant
Admiralty Bay
☎ 458-3800
Seafood and continental $-$$

The Green Boley
Belmont Beach
☎ 458-3247
Snacks and fast food $

Harpoon Saloon
Port Elizabeth
☎ 458-3272
Sea food, Creole and continental $-$$. A good place to hang out.

Julie's Guest House
Back Street
Port Elizabeth
☎ 458-3304
West Indian and Creole specialities $-$$

Keegan's
Lower Bay
☎ 458-3530
West Indian specialities $-$$

Le Petit Jardin
Back Street
Port Elizabeth
☎ 458-3318
French and international. Good wine list. $$

Mac's Pizzeria and Bake Shop
Belmont Beach
☎ 458-3474 $

Maranne's Ice Cream
Belmont Beach
☎ 458-3041
Ice creams $

Ocean View Restaurant
Friendship Bay Resort
☎ 458-3222
West Indian seafood and International with good wine list $-$$

Old Fig Tree
Belmont Beach
☎ 458-3201. Seafood and West Indian specialities $-$$

Old Fort Restaurant
Old Fort Hotel
☎ 458-3440
West Indian and Creole $$

opposite: Admiralty Bay, Bequia

TOURING & EXPLORING THE GRENADINES

Plantation House Restaurant
Belmont
☎ 458-3425
International $$

The Port Hole
Port Elizabeth
☎ 458-3458
West Indian and Creole specialities $-$$

Spicy 'N Herby Beach Bar
Friendship Bay Resort
☎ 458-3222
West Indian, seafood and light meals. Lobster BBQs Tuesdays. $-$$

Spring on Bequia Hotel Restaurant
Spring
☎ 458-3414
Seafood and Creole specialities $$

Theresa's
Lower Bay
☎ 458-3802
West Indian specialities $-$$

The Whaleboner
Port Elizabeth
☎ 458-3233
West Indian & Creole specialities $-$$

Canouan

Anchor Inn
Grand Bay
☎ 458-8568.
West Indian and seafood $$

Canouan Beach Hotel
☎ 458-8888
West Indian and seafood $$

Crystal Sands Beach Hotel
☎ 458-8309
West Indian and international $$

Palapa Restaurant
☎ 458-8044
Seafood/Italian $-$$

Tamarind Beach Hotel
☎ 458-8044
West Indian and seafood $-$$

Villa Le Bijou
☎ 458-8025
Seafood and Creole specialities $$

Mustique

Basil's Bar and Raft Restaurant
Britannia Bay
☎ 458-4621
Seafood, especially lobster and shrimp, and local specialities. Weekly barbecue and jump up. $-$$

Mayreau

Denis' Hideaway
☎ 458-8594
Guest house and restaurant serving seafood and West Indian specialities.

Union Island

Anchorage Yacht Club Restaurant
☎ 458-8221
French and Creole specialities
$$-$$$

Clifton Beach Hotel
☎ 458-8235
West Indian specialities $$

Eagle's Nest
☎ 458-8319
Snacks and local specialities $

Lambi's
☎ 458-8549
Seafood $-$$

Sunny Grenadines
☎ 458-8327
Seafood and international $$

T & N
☎ 458-8207
West Indian specialities and seafood $-$$

Traveller's Tips

Arrivals, Entry & Customs	111
Accommodation	111
Airlines	124
American Express	125
Banks	125
Beauty Salons & Hairdressers	126
Camping	126
Car Rental	126
Churches	127
Currency & Credit Cards	128
Departure Tax	128
Disabled Facilities	128
Dress Code	128
Electricity	129
Embassies & Consulates	129
Emergency Telephone Numbers	129
Essential Things to Pack	129
Fishing	129
Gambling	130
Health	130
Hospitals	130
Hurricanes	131
Language	131
Lost Property	131
Media	131
Music	132
Nightlife	132
Personal Insurance	132
Pets	132
Pharmacies	132
Photography	133
Police	133
Ports	134
Post Offices	134
Public Holidays & Festivals	134
Public Toilets	134
Restaurants	134
Security	135
Service Charges & Taxes	135
Sightseeing	135
Sport	136
Telephones	139
Time	139
Tipping	140
Tourist Information Offices	140
Tour Operators	141
Weddings	141
Yacht Charter & Private Moorings	142

ARRIVAL, ENTRY REQUIREMENTS & CUSTOMS

An immigration form has to be filled in and presented on arrival. The form requires you to say where you will be staying on the island, and if you plan to move around, put down the first hotel you will be staying at. The immigration form is in two parts, one of which is stamped and returned to you in your passport. You must retain this until departure when the slip is retrieved as you check in at the airport.

British, American and Canadian citizens staying for less than six months, do not need a passport provided they have proof of citizenship, such as a birth certificate. Visitors from the United States and Canada can enter on an ID card but must have valid return tickets. It is, however, a good idea to travel with your passport, and citizens from all other countries require one. Visas are not required. You may also be asked to show that you have a return ticket before being admitted.

If travelling on business, a letter confirming this, may prove helpful in speeding your way through customs, especially if travelling with samples.

Having cleared immigration, you will have to go through customs, and it is quite usual to have to open your luggage for inspection. If you have expensive cameras, binoculars, jewellery etc it is a good idea to travel with a photocopy of the receipt. The duty free allowance entering the island is 200 cigarettes or 250 grams of tobacco or 50 cigars, and one quart of spirits or wine.

You may be asked to pay a deposit on some of your personal items such as radios and electrical goods, which is refunded when you leave, providing you still have them in your possession. Customs and Excise offices are open Monday to Friday between 8am and 4pm, and on Saturday between 8.30am and noon.

ACCOMMODATION

St Vincent and the Grenadines has a wide range of accommodation to suit all tastes and pockets, from the luxurious all-inclusive resorts to inns, and modest guest houses, self-catering apartments and beach cottages.

If you want to eat out and

opposite: Argyle Nature Resort, on the east coast of St Vincent

explore quite a lot, it may pay to stay in a hotel offering part board, or one of the many inns on the island, some of them converted plantation homes, and generally offering excellent value for money.

There are also apartments, holiday villas and beach cottages available for rent offering you the privacy of your own accommodation and the flexibility to eat in or out.

Some terms: MAP stands for Modified American Plan, ie breakfast and dinner are included. EP or European Plan means bed only and no meals. CP is Continental Plan which is bed and breakfast, and AP for American Plan, means room and all meals.

Prices quoted by hotels are for rooms, whether one or two people are sharing, and you may find it difficult to get a reduction if you are travelling alone, but you might be successful if you ask. Prices, unless clearly stated, do not usually include the 7 per cent Government tax and there may be a 10 per cent service charge as well.

- $ = inexpensive accommodation
- $$ = moderate accommodation
- $$$ = de-luxe accommodation

Accommodation A-Z

St Vincent

Hotels

Argyle Nature Resort
$-$$ CP. 6 rooms.
Overlooking Argyle Beach.
☎ 458-0992
A small resort overlooking the beach with pool, small restaurant and beautifully furnished rooms. Facilities for windsurfing and horse riding.

Beachcombers Hotel
$ CP. 12 rooms.
Villa Beach
☎ 458-4283
Attractive terraced villas and self-catering en-suite rooms, set in tropical gardens which run down to the beach. Waterside bar and restaurant.

Cobblestone Inn
$ CP. 19 rooms.
Kingstown
☎ 456-1937
This historic inn was built in 1814 as a sugar warehouse. It has been very attractively restored and converted and all rooms have en-suite facilities. It also has many lovely features such as the original cobblestone walkways and arches. It has two restaurants and two bars, and is a five-minute drive to the beaches.

— TRAVELLERS' TIPS —

Coconut Beach Hotel
$ EP. 9 rooms.
Indian Bay
☎ 457-4900
The hotel is right on the beach and only ten minutes from town. All rooms have en-suite facilities. It has a water's edge restaurant and bar.

Emerald Valley Resort and Casino
$ EP. 12 cottages
☎ 456-7140
Set in 12 acres of tropical gardens in the valley and overlooking the river, this hotel centres around the casino, pool-side restaurant and bar. There is often live music and barbecues, and a unique nine-hole golf course.

Grand View Beach Hotel
$$-$$$ EP. 20 rooms
Villa Point
☎ 458-4811
This family-run hotel is set in 8 acres of beautiful landscaped gardens with wonderful views of the Grenadines, and overlooks a quiet little beach. The large en suite rooms are very attractively furnished, and the hotel has a restaurant featuring the finest of local produce, bar, pool with swim up bar, fitness centre with massage and sauna, tennis, squash, snorkelling and watersports facilities. It also has conference facilities.

Haddon Hotel
$ EP. 17 rooms.
Kingstown
☎ 456-1897
This friendly hotel is close to downtown Kingstown, only five minutes from the airport and ten minutes from the beach. It offers ten executive self-contained suites, and its restaurant is noted for specialising in the local cuisine. Self-drive cars and tennis are available.

Heron Hotel
$ CP. 15 rooms.
Bay Street
Kingstown
☎ 457-1631
A very comfortable and friendly bed-and-breakfast hotel with en suite facilities, close to the centre of town, and only a short drive to the beaches. There is a friendly bar and restaurant specialising in local dishes, and overlooking the courtyard where breakfast and light lunches are served. Reservations required for dinner Monday-Friday.

Indian Bay Beach Hotel & Apartments
$ CP, EP, MAP 13 rooms.
Indian Bay Beach
☎ 458-4001
Situated by the white sands of Indian Bay, the hotel has a restaurant that specialises in seafood

and local cuisine. There is also a bar. Watersports are available nearby, and there is wondeful snorkelling in the underwater gardens just offshore. Boat rides, wind surfing and water skiing facilities are also available.

Lagoon Hotel and Marina
$$-$$$ EP. 19 rooms.
Blue Lagoon
☎ 458-4308
A first-class hotel with nineteen de-luxe en-suite rooms beside the Caribbean Sailing Yachts marina. It has a restaurant and bar and two-tiered swimming pool. Facilities include snorkelling, wind surfing and daily skippered sailing trips to Bequia and Mustique. Also conference facilities.

Petit Byahaut
$$ AP 7 rooms.
Petit Byahaut Bay
☎ 457-7008
Set in a 50-acre valley which runs from the beach and only accessible by boat. Seven luxury permanent tents provide accommodation. Great base for hiking, diving, fishing, nature watching or getting away from it all.

Sunset Shores Hotel
$$ EP. 32 rooms.
Villa Beach
☎ 458-4411
This beachfront hotel has en suite rooms, many with their own private patios. The courtyard, set in lush gardens, includes a covered bar and pool and the restaurant specialises in seafood. Watersports and snorkelling are available, and the hotel also has excellent conference facilities.

Villa Lodge Hotel
$$ EP. 10 rooms.
Villa Point
☎ 458-4641
The hotel is set in wonderful tropical gardens on the hillside overlooking Indian Bay, although it is less than 200 feet to the water's edge. The restaurant is noted for seafood and its barbecued steaks, and there is a cocktail bar and luxurious pool. There is a barbecue with live music on Saturday nights. The beach is close by and watersports and snorkelling are available.

Young Island Resort
$$$ AP. 29 cottages.
Young Island
☎ 458-4826
Young Island is just 200 yards and about as close to paradise as many people will get. The 35-acre island is privately owned and its white sandy beaches are fringed with palms. There are twenty-nine cottages all with marvellous views, set among the trees which afford privacy. There are three restaurants, two bars, watersports,

Wallilabou

The beautifully furnished chalets at the Plantation Hotel, Bequia

snorkelling, scuba and floodlit tennis, and the resort has its own vessels, including two 44ft yachts, which are available to guests. Cocktail parties with music are held every Thursday evening at Fort Duvernette just across the water.

Apartments

Belleville Apartments
$ EP. 8 apartments.
Villa
☎ 458-4776.
Close to the beach, all units have cooking facilities although there is a restaurant.

Breezeville Apartments
$$ EP. 8 rooms.
Villa Point
☎ 458-4004
Studio apartments set amid scenery and with magnificent panoramic views over the mountains and Indian Bay Beach less than 100 yards away. There is a bar and restaurant, pool, and nearby tennis, squash and a fitness centre.

Macedonia Rock Hotel
$ EP. 21 rooms.
Cane Hall
☎ 458-4076
Close to the airport, the hotel has some facilities for the handicapped, plus restaurant and bar.

New Montrose Apartments
$$ EP. 20 small, self-contained apartments.
Kingstown
☎ 457-0172

Ratho Mill Apartments
15 apartments.
Ratho Mill
☎ 458-4849
The building with comfortable, self-contained apartments, overlooks the palm fringed bay, and has restaurant and bar.

Ricks Apartments
$ CP. 12 rooms.
Cane Hall
☎ 456-1242.

Ridgeview Terrace Apartments
$ EP. 5 apartments.
Ratho Mill
☎ 456-1615
Close to the beach and airport, the apartments all have private balconies and fine views.

Tranquility Beach Apartments
$ EP. 12 units.
Indian Bay Beach
☎ 458-4021
All units have balconies with views of the bay. There is a bar and restaurant. Scenic tours and tours of the Botanical Gardens available, as well as snorkelling, and mountain climbing. Cooks available on request.

Umbrella Beach Hotel
$ EP. 9 apartments.
Villa Beach
☎ 4589-4651
On the ocean front with restaurants, bars and watersports available close by.

Guest Houses

Adams Guest House
$ CP. 6 apartments.
Arnos Vale
☎ 458-4656
Self contained apartments one mile from the beach, with meals available on request. Watersports are available and island and boat tours can be arranged.

Bella Vista Inn
$ EP. 6 rooms.
Kingstown Park
☎ 457-2757
A small inn in its own gardens and overlooking the town. It has a small restaurant and bar.

Highfield Guest House
$ EP. 9 rooms.
Lowmans, Leeward
☎ 457-7563

Kingstown Park Guest House
$ EP. 20 rooms.
Kingstown Park
☎ 456-1532
In a 200-year-old Colonial-style plantation house with a restaurant specialising in Creole cuisine.

Kingstown Park Inn
$ CP. 8 rooms.
Kingstown
☎ 457-2964
New bed-and-breakfast establishment close to Downtown with restaurant and bar.

The Moon Guest House
$ EP. 16 rooms.
Amos Vale
☎ 458-4656

Ocean View Inn
$ CP. 5 rooms.
Villa Point
☎ 457-4332
Small, friendly bed-and-breakfast inn is set in lush, tropical gardens, just three minutes from Indian Bay beach. A variety of day tours, watersports and boat trips can be arranged.

Paradise Inn
$ EP. 4 units.
Villa
☎ 457-4795
Close to Villa Beach and set in tropical gardens, this small inn offers rooms and self-contained apartments. It has a bar and restaurant noted for its local specialities as well as Continental cuisine.

Sea Breeze Guest House
$ EP. 6 rooms.
Amos Vale
☎ 458-4969

Close to both the airport and beaches, with a snackette next door and supermarket closeby.

The Grenadines — Bequia

Bequia Beach Club
$-$$ MAP. 10 bungalows.
Friendship Bay
☎ 458-3248
The terrace bungalows, all furnished to a high standard, form their own little village and are close to the beach. There is daily maid service. There is a bar and restaurant, and facilities on offer include diving school with snorkelling and scuba, surfing, sailing and fishing, and island tours. Monday night is barbecue night.

Blue Tropic Hotel
$ CP. 10 rooms.
Friendship Bay
☎ 458-3573.
This new apartment hotel — all rooms have private balconies with magnificent sea views — is set on a small hill overlooking the bay yet only a minute's walk from the beach. The hotel is noted for its Flame Tree garden restaurant and also has a friendly bar. Facilities include the free use of bicycles for exploring the island.

Creole Garden Hotel
$ MAP. 4 rooms.
Lower Bay
☎ 458-3154
The hotel stands at the end of the bay with great harbour and sea views. New studio apartments have their own private terrace and garden area. There is a bar and restaurant.

De Reef Apartments
$-$$ EP. 5 apartments.
Lower Bay
☎ 458-3447
These new, well-equipped, self-contained apartments are set in their own gardens and are just a few yards from the beach. There is a beach bar and waterside restaurant that specialises in sea food seven days a week. Sunday lunches at De Reef are becoming something of an island occasion.

Fairmont Apartments
$-$$ CP. 3 apartments.
Belmont
☎ 458-4037
Well-equipped apartments with maid service, in a delightful garden setting in Belmont overlooking Admiralty Bay. The terraced apartments, set well back off the road, have large balconies and are surrounded by trees.

Frangipani
$ EP. 16 rooms.
Port Elizabeth
☎ 458-3255
A charming small hotel set in colourful gardens and with fabulous views over Admiralty Bay,

and noted for its lively Thursday night barbecue and jump-up. The main house is built in classic Westindian Gingerbread style, and there is also accommodation in the attractive wood and stone cottages set around the garden. There is an open-air bar and restaurant noted for sea-food and local cuisine, and facilities include boat trips, diving, snorkelling, scuba, organised hikes, guided tours, watersports and tennis. The hotel has its own small boutique.

Friendship Bay Hotel
$$ CP. 27 en-suite rooms.
Friendship
☎ 458-3222
A lively comfortable hotel beside a long stretch of sandy beach, and noted for its well-stocked bar and Spicy 'n Herby Restaurant which serves an interesting variety of Caribbean and Creole dishes with hints of Swedish and Oriental cuisine. There are daily specials. There is lots of live music and the hotel is famous for its regular Saturday night jump-ups. There is also a beach bar, tennis, volleyball court, diving and snorkelling, sailing, windsurfing and water skiing. Yacht charters, boat trips and island tours can also be arranged.

Gingerbread Apartments
$ EP. 3 units.
Admiralty Bay
☎ 458-3800
The apartments are on Admiralty Bay and only a short walk from Port Elizabeth. The verandah, hanging balcony and eaves are a mass of gingerbread ornamentation. There is a restaurant and bar, as well as an open air cafe and store. Facilities for tennis, snorkelling, scuba and sunfish.

Hibiscus Apartments
$ EP. 4 apartments.
Union Vale
☎ 458-3316
The self-contained apartments are conveniently situated close to Port Elizabeth and the beaches at Admiralty Bay on the west coast and Spring Bay on the east coast, all about a ten-minute walk away.

Julie's Guest House
$ AP. 20 rooms.
Port Elizabeth
☎ 458-3304
A delightful guest house offering very friendly service. All rooms have their own balcony with glorious views. It has a dining room specialising in local dishes and bar, and it holds barbecues and beach picnics to the accompaniment of steel bands. It can arrange watersports, boat trips and island tours.

Keegan's Guest House
$ AP. 11 rooms and 2 apartments.
Lower Bay
☎ 458-3530
The guest house is almost on the white sand beach and has a restaurant and bar.

Kings Ville Apartments
$-$$ EP. 8 apartments.
Lower Bay
☎ 458-3404
Close to the white sand beach at Lower Bay, it has six self-contained cottage-style apartments set in tropical gardens.

Lower Bay Guest House
$ EP. 8 rooms.
Lower Bay
☎ 458-3675

The Old Fig Tree Guest House
$ EP. 6 rooms.
Admiralty Bay
☎ 458-3201.
On the beach and close to the jetty. Offers light lunches and dinners on request.

Old Fort Country Inn
$$ EP. 6 rooms.
Mount Pleasant
☎ 458-3440
This former estate house built on top of the hill 450ft above sea level, has been curiously rebuilt to resemble a fortified medieval block house. The en-suite rooms are large and comfortable, and the house is set in magnificent gardens. There is a restaurant and open air bar, and boat trips and island tours can be arranged.

Plantation House Hotel
$$-$$$ AP, EP. 45 luxury rooms and cottages.
Belmont
☎ 458-3425
An excellent resort which has recently been extended and upgraded. Set in more than ten acres of tropical gardens there are twenty-seven beautifully furnished and appointed cottages all with verandahs and sea views, and thirteen garden cottages, as well as large rooms in the Colonial-style main building. The hotel has an extensive beach frontage overlooked by an informal eating area and bar, while the main restaurant offers the best dining on the island. The chef, imported from Europe, even grows many of his own vegetables and herbs to ensure that only the freshest of ingredients are used. The hotel is also the home of Dive Bequia, which operates from headquarters by the beach. Other facilities include boutique, tennis, pool, water skiing, windsurfing and sailing. Boat trips, charters and island tours can be arranged.

Spring on Bequia
$-$$$ EP, MAP. 10 rooms.
Spring
☎ 458-3414
A delightful, small hotel set in the grounds of the historic Spring Plantation established more than 250 years ago. Some of the guest rooms are built on the foundations of the original great house, and all have their own private patio. There is an open-air bar and restaurant, extensive beach, freshwater pool, tennis and snorkelling.

Village Apartments
$ EP. 8 apartments.
Lower Bay
☎ 456-4960
The self-contained apartments overlook Admiralty Bay and are only a short walk from the beach. Snorkelling, scuba, sailing and yacht charters can be arranged, as well as island tours.

Bequia Villa Rentals
☎ 458-3393
Friendship Bay Villa Rentals
☎ 458-3222
These two companies offer a large number of villas and apartments for holiday lettings.

Canouan

Anchor Inn Guest House
$ MAP. 4 rooms.
☎ 458-8560.

Canouan Beach Hotel
$$-$$$ AP. 43 rooms.
☎ 458-8888
This resort hotel is right beside the white sandy beach set in tropical flower gardens, with lush hillsides behind. Most of the comfortably furnished rooms have ocean views. Bar and restaurant. Facilities include tennis and table tennis, volleyball, watersports, scuba, snorkelling and trips on the hotel's catamaran. Live entertainment and dancing twice weekly.

Crystal Apartments Restaurant and Bar
$ MAP. 2 double apartments.
☎ 458-8309

Tamarind Beach Hotel and Yacht Club
$$$ MAP. 45 rooms.
☎ 458-8044
All inclusive luxury resort with fine cuisine. Excellent watersports facilities and cruising.

Villa Le Bijou
$$ MAP. 10 rooms.
☎ 458-8025
A small guest house on the hill with beautiful views of the other Grenadines, and only five minutes from the beach.

Mayreau

Dennis' Hideaway
$ EP. 3 rooms.
☎ 458-8594
A small, very comfortable, very friendly little guesthouse with restaurant.

Salt Whistle Bay
$$-$$$ 27 rooms.
☎ Boatphone 458-8444
Luxury little hotel on the beach with delightfully furnished, en-suite rooms and bungalows. There is an open-air restaurant and bar, and facilities include watersports, snorkelling, scuba, volleyball and table tennis, and fishing and sailing trips can be arranged.

Mustique

Cotton House
$$-$$$ 24 rooms.
☎ 456-4777
A delightful eighteenth-century stone and coral building surrounded by guest cottages. The main building was originally a cotton store house now converted to a luxury hotel. Restaurant and bar, and facilities include swmming pool, tennis, horseback riding and watersports. Boat trips and island tours arranged.

Firefly House
$$ CP. 4 rooms.
☎ 456-3414
A delightful private villa overlooking Britannia Bay offering rooms with breakfast. It is two minutes from the beach; watersports and tennis avalable.

Mustique Company Villas
☎ 458-4621
Can help with rentals.

Palm Island (Prune Island)

Palm Island Beach Club
$$-$$$ AP. 24 rooms.
☎ 458-8824
You can take your pick from five beaches on this 130-acre private island. Excellent accommodation in the beach club or in the surrounding villas. All rooms have en-suite facilities and patio, and the restaurant is noted for its seafood dishes, especially lobster, and Creole cuisine. Barbecues are held regularly. Tennis, fitness centre, watersports, scuba, snorkelling, fishing, sailing and cruising.

Petit St Vincent

Petit St Vincent Resort
$$$ AP. 22 cottages.
☎ 458-8801
A 113-acre private island resort surrounded by fabulous sandy beaches. The island is four miles from Union Island which has the nearest airstrip. Luxury accommodation in spacious cottages set

Kingstown, St Vincent, has branches of several international banks

among the tropical gardens. The restaurant has a deservedly high reputation, and there is a piano bar. Facilities include shop, floodlit tennis, badminton, croquet, watersports, scuba, snorkelling, sailing, deep sea and reef fishing and diving. Self-drive cars and boats also available.

Union Island

Anchorage Yacht Club
$$-$$$ CP, MAP, AP. 10 rooms.
Clifton
☎ 458-8221

A splendid resort with great rooms or your own bungalow and fabulous views of the neighbouring Grenadines. The club, with its own airstrip, is based on the water's edge with excellent facilities for visiting yachts and white sand beaches for guests. The restaurant is noted for its French and speciality local dishes. There is also a lively terrace bar, much frequented by visiting yachtsmen, and the club is noted for its steel band jump-ups. It also has its own boutiques, and offers mini-cruises, sport and line fishing and diving.

Cays Apartments
$-$$ EP 5 apartments.
Richmond Bay
☎ 456-2221

Clifton Beach Hotel
$$-$$$ MAP. 25 rooms.
Clifton
☎ 458-8235

Stay in the hotel, guest house, or one of the apartments and cottages all close to the sea and the superb beach. There is a waterside restaurant which specialises in the local cuisine, although some rooms have kitchenettes for self catering, and you can enjoy a snack on the terrace overlooking the jetty, or a drink in the carousel-shaped bar. Watersports, snorkelling, and shopping are available nearby.

Lambi's Guest House
$ EP. 14 rooms.
Clifton
☎ 458-8549

A lively place during the season with a steel band entertaining dinner guests in the restaurant. The guest house has fourteen double rooms, its own dinghy dock, and mini-mart.

Sunny Grenadines
$ CP, MAP. 14 rooms.
Clifton
☎ 458-8327

This charming, comfortable little hotel is on the beach at Clifton Harbour. The restaurant specialises in seafood and local cuisine. Facilities include watersports, scuba, snorkelling, sailing, cruising and island tours. It has a conference room.

AIRLINES

Air Carriacou
☎ 444-2898

Air Martinique
St Vincent
☎ 458-4528
Union Island
☎ 458-8826

BWIA International
In the US ☎ 1-800-JET-BWIA
(1-800-538-2942)
In the UK ☎ 0171-839-9333

British Airways
☎ 457-1821

Carib Express
☎ 456-5075

LIAT
Kingstown
☎ 457-1821
E. T. Joshua Airport
☎ 458-4841
Union Island Airport
☎ 458-8230.

Mustique Airways
☎ 458-4380

SVG Air
☎ 456-5610

AMERICAN EXPRESS

Local representatives are
New Bank
Bay Street
Kingstown
☎ 457-1411
Caribbean International Travel
Granby Street
Kingstown
☎ 457-1841

BANKS

Banks are open Monday to Friday 8am to 3pm, and to 5pm on Fridays. Banks are generally closed at weekends and on public holidays. There are banking facilities at E. T. Joshua Airport from Monday to Saturday 7am-5pm, with longer hours over Christmas, Easter and Carnival. Banks are:

Barclays Bank
Halifax Street
Kingstown
☎ 456-1706
Bequia
☎ 458-3215.

Canadian Imperial Bank of Commerce
Halifax Street
Kingstown
☎ 457-1587

Caribbean Banking Corporation
South River Road
Kingstown
☎ 456-1501

First St Vincent Bank
Granby Street
Kingstown
☎ 456-1873

National Commercial Bank of St Vincent
Grenville Street
Kingstown
☎ 457-1844
Also at Halifax Street, Kingstown, E. T. Joshua Airport, and on Bequia and Union Island.

New Bank
Bay Street
Kingstown
☎ 457-1411

St Vincent Co-operative Bank
Middle Street
Kingstown
☎ 456-1894

Scotia Bank (Bank of Nova Scotia)
Halifax Street
Kingstown
☎ 457-1601

BEAUTY SALONS & HAIRDRESSERS

There are several beauty salons and hairdressers in Kingstown.

CAMPING

There are no camping facilities on St Vincent and sleeping out, especially on the beach, is not permitted.

CAR RENTAL

Cars and four-wheel-drive vehicles can be hired and provide the best way of exploring the island. If you plan to go at peak periods, it is best to hire your vehicle in advance through your travel agent. Cars can be hired, however, at airports, hotels or car hire offices on the island.

Hire car rates range from US$ 300 to 400 a week depending on the type of vehicle and the rental company. Average daily rates are around US$65 and this does not include insurance, which costs an additional US$15-20 a day.

A temporary St Vincent driving licence is required, and can be obtained on production of your current driving licence or a valid international driving licence, on arrival at the airport, the police station in Bay Street, the motor licensing authority in Halifax Street (open Monday to Friday 9am to 3pm), or the car hire office. It costs EC$40.

Hire companies on St Vincent include:

Avis Rent-a-Car
Amos Vale
☎ 458-5610

David's Auto Clinic
Upper Sion Hill
Kingstown
☎ 456-4026

Hertz
Grenville Street
Kingstown
☎ 456-1743

Kim's Rentals
Grenville Street
Kingstown
☎ 456-1884

Star Garage
Grenville Street
Kingstown
☎ 456-1743

Sunshine Auto Rentals
Amos Vale
☎ 456-5380

UNICO Auto Rentals
Amos Vale
☎ 456-5744

Scooters can be rented, together with crash helmets, from:

J. G. Agencies
☎ 456-1409

Sailors Cycle Centre
☎ 457-1712.

Rules of the road

DRIVE ON THE LEFT. The roads are generally good and there are substantial road improvements under way. In rural areas, however, you need to look out for potholes, fallen branches, coconuts on the road, etc. Do not speed because you never know what may be round the next corner. The further north one travels from Kingstown, either on the east or west coast, the narrower and bendier the roads become. Many interior roads and in the north are best negotiated using four-wheel-drive vehicles. Always check the suitability of the roads for your vehicle before setting out.

The islanders love of cricket encourages them to play at every opportunity, and the road makes an ideal pitch!

Seat belts are not compulsory but is is advisable to wear them at all times. The speed limit is 30mph in towns and there is no reason to go very much faster out of town, because you will not fully appreciate the scenery.

Drinking and driving is against the law, and there are heavy penalties if convicted, especially if it resulted in an accident.

Avoid clearly marked 'no parking' zones or you might pick up a ticket, but parking generally does not pose a problem.

If you have an accident or breakdown during the day, call your car hire company, so make sure you have the telephone number with you. They will usually send out a mechanic or a replacement vehicle. If you are stuck at night make sure the car is off the road, lock the vehicle and call a taxi to take you back to your hotel. Report the problem to the car hire company or the police as soon as possible.

CHURCHES

The main religions are Anglican, Methodist and Roman Catholic. Other denominations represented are Baptist, Pentecostal, Salvation Army, Seventh Day Adventist, Streams of Power and Baha'i Fath. There are daily early morning services (6am) at St. George's Anglican Cathedral, in Kingstown, while a Folk Mass is held every Saturday evening at the Roman Catholic Church, as well as other services and masses during the week. Times of services can be obtained from hotel staff, tourist offices and so on.

CURRENCY & CREDIT CARDS

The official currency on the island is the East Caribbean dollar although US dollars are accepted almost everywhere. At the time of writing the exchange rate was US$ to EC$2.65, and £1 to EC$4. EC$ come in the following denomination notes: 5, 10, 20, 50 and 100, with 1c, 2c, 5c, 10c, 25c, 50c and one dollar coins.

The banks offer a fixed, and generally a better rate of exchange than hotels and shops. Travellers cheques, preferably in US dollars, are also accepted in hotels and large stores, and all major credit cards can be used in hotels, large stores and restaurants. They are also accepted by tour operators and car hire companies.

Note: Always make certain that you know what currency you are dealing in when arranging a taxi ride, guide, charter and so on. First establish the currency (either EC$ or US$) and then agree a price. It could save a lot of arguments later on.

Always have a few small denomination notes, either US$1 or EC$5 notes for tips.

DEPARTURE TAX

There is a departure tax of EC$20 for all passengers leaving the island.

DISABLED FACILITIES

There are facilities for the disabled at some of the larger hotels, but not much elsewhere.

DRESS CODE

Casual is the keyword but you can be as smart or as cool as you like. Swimwear is fine for the beach and pool areas, but cover up a little for the street and shopping. Sandals are necessary for the beach as the sand gets very hot. Wear a hat if planning to be out in the sun for a long time. Dressing up for dinner can be fun, but I do not know of anywhere where ties have to be worn. If you plan to do a lot of walking, especially on interior trails, bring sturdy, non slip footwear, a waterproof jacket and a light jumper as it can get chilly at altitude out of the sun.

ELECTRICITY

The usual electricity supply is 220 volts, 50 cycles alternating current, and most sockets take UK-style three-pin plugs, although most hotels have 110v plugs for electric razors. Some hotels, however, also have 110 volt supplies which are suitable for US appliances. Adaptors are generally available at the hotels, or can be purchased if you do not travel with your own. Petit St Vincent has an electrical supply of 110v 60 cycle.

EMBASSIES & CONSULATES

British High Commission
Grenville Street
Kingstown
☎ 457-1701

Consulate of the Netherlands
St Clair House
Melville Street
Kingstown
☎ 457-2677

French Consulate
Middle Street
Kingstown
☎ 456-1615

Embassy of Venezuela
Granby Street
Kingstown
☎ 456-1374

EMERGENCY TELEPHONE NUMBERS

For Police, Fire and Ambulance dial 999
Coastguard 457-1211/4578

ESSENTIAL THINGS TO PACK

Sun tan cream, sunglasses, sun hat, camera (and lots of film), insect repellant, binoculars if interested in bird watching and wildlife, and a small torch in case of power failures.

FISHING

Fishing is an island-wide pursuit, and many islanders will fish for hours from harbour walls, from the beach or river side. Deep sea and game fishing is mostly for blue marlin and tuna which can weigh up to 1,000lb, wahoo and white marlin, which can weigh more than 100lb and the fighting sailfish. Snapper, grouper, bonito, dorado and barracuda can all be kept close to shore. Licences are not necessary for pleasure fishing, although some areas are off-limits. You can get details from the Fisheries Department in the Government Offices building in Kingstown (☎ 456-2738). Permission is also required from the department if you want to use a spear gun. There are a number of boats available for fishing trips, and these can usually be arranged directly with the fisherman.

GAMBLING

There is a casino at the Emerald Valley Hotel and Casino on St Vincent
☎ 456-7140

HEALTH

There are no serious health problems although visitors should take precautions against the sun and mosquitoes, both of which can ruin your holiday. Immunisation is not required unless travelling from an infected area within six days of arrival.

All hotels have doctors either resident or on call.
Note: Drinking water from the tap is safe although bottled mineral and distilled water is widely available.

Irritating Insects & Other Hazards
Mosquitoes can be a problem almost anywhere. In your room, burn mosquito coils or use one of the many electrical plug-in devices which burn an insect repelling tablet. Mosquitoes are not so much of a problem on or near the beaches because of onshore winds, but they may well bite you as you enjoy an open-air evening meal. Use a good insect repellant, particularly if you are planning trips inland such as walking in the rain forests.

Lemon grass can be found growing naturally, and a handful of this in your room is also a useful mosquito deterrent.

Sand flies can be a problem on the beach. Despite their tiny size they can give you a nasty bite. And, ants abound, so make sure you check the ground carefully before sitting down otherwise you might get bitten, and the bites can itch for days. Several creams are available to relieve itchiness from insect bites and Bay Rum is a good remedy when dabbed on the skin.

Sea Urchins are common so be careful to avoid stepping on them and getting painful spines embedded in your feet which can cause serious irritation and may get infected.

HOSPITALS

There is a general hospital in Kingstown off the Leeward Highway (☎ 456-1185), with X-ray, dental and eye clinics, and smaller facilities at Georgetown on the east coast (☎ 458-6652), and Chateaubelair on the west coast. There is also an infants' hospital at Mount Bentinck in Georgetown. (☎ 458-6244). There are also a number of health clinics on the islands, including:

The Bayside Medical Clinic
Lower Bay Street
Kingstown
☎ 456-1127

Botanic Clinic
New Montrose
☎ 457-9781

Campden Park Clinic
Campden Park
☎ 456-1640

Clare Valley Clinic
Clare Valley
☎ 457-8390

Medical Associates Clinic
Middle Street
Kingstown
☎ 457-2598

Rampersaud Clinic
Grenville Street
Kingstown
☎ 457-1873

There is a small casualty hospital in Port Elizabeth, Bequia, and clinics on Mustique and Union Island.

HURRICANES

St Vincent is fortunate in that it has suffered less from hurricanes than many other Caribbean islands, although Hurricane Allen did devastating damage when it came ashore in 1980. The hurricane season is between August and early October, with September the most likely month for tropical storms, although almost all of these pass safely well north of the island.

LANGUAGE

The official language spoken is English, although most people also speak the local patois.

LOST PROPERTY

Report lost property as soon as possible to your hotel or the nearest police station.

MEDIA

There are four weekly newspapers and the Government runs a free public library system. There are also the free and very useful tourist publications *Discover St Vincent and the Grenadines* which give details about what's on, and are full of interesting island information. There are two publications; for St Vincent and for Bequia.

The island has a television station and a radio station broadcasting on AM 705khz.

MUSIC

Music is a way of life and the philosophy is the louder it is played, the better. Cars, mini-van buses and open doorways all seem to blast music out, and once the music starts it goes on for hours. When the islanders party, it often lasts all night.

NIGHTLIFE

Most people get up early in St Vincent and go to bed early, so there are not too many nightclubs. Most hotels provide some evening entertainment with steelbands, local folk troups, etc. There are also beach barbecues and some notable regular jump-ups at one or two hotels. In St Vincent recommended nightspots include the Aquatic Club, The Attic in Melville Street, Spotlight Stadium, Philos and the Touch Entertainment Centre. On Bequia and the other Grenadines, hotels provide most of the entertainment, but on Bequia try Crescent Beach or Harpoon Saloon, and ask around, and on Mustique, pop in to Basil's Bar.

PERSONAL INSURANCE & MEDICAL COVER

Make sure you have adequate personal insurance and medical cover. If you need to call out a doctor or have medical treatment, you will probably have to pay for it at the time, so keep all receipts to reclaim on your insurance.

PETS

Pets aboard yachts must stay on the vessel at all times. Pets from Britain, Australia and New Zealand may be admitted into the country if in possession of the relevant veterinary documents and animal health certificates. Check with the Government Veterinary Officer ☎ 456-1111.

PHARMACIES

If you are taking drugs and medicines prescribed by your doctor, it is a good idea to bring enough to last you throughout your stay. Also bring a copy of your prescription, or a letter from your doctor, to prove the drugs are yours, and this will also help you replace them if you lose them.

Pharmacies in Kingstown include:

Davis Drug Mart
Corner of Tyrrell & McCoy Streets
☎ 456-1174

Deane's Pharmacy
Middle Street
☎ 456-2877

Gaymes Pharmacy
Grenville Street
☎ 456-1861

Grant T Geddes Pharmacy
Middle Street
☎ 456-1325

Medix Pharmacy
Grenville Street
☎ 456-2989

Pharmco
Tyrrell Street
☎ 456-1797

Reliance Pharmacy
Halifax Street
☎ 456-1734

Royal Pharmacy
Grenville Street
☎ 456-1817

Thomas Matthew Pharmaceuticals
Grenville Street
☎ 456-2133

There is also

Mespo Pharmacy
Mesopotamia
☎ 458-1743

Bequia Pharmacy,
Port Elizabeth, Bequia
☎ 458-3296

PHOTOGRAPHY

The intensity of the sun can play havoc with film, especially if photographing near water or white sand. Compensate for the brightness or your photographs will be over exposed and wishy-washy. The heat can damage film so store reels in a box or bag in the hotel fridge. Protect your camera if on the beach, as a single grain of sand can jam a camera. It is very easy to get 'click happy' in the Caribbean, but be tactful when taking photographs. Many islanders are shy or simply fed up with being photographed, and others will insist on a small payment. You will have to decide whether the picture is worth it, but if a person declines to have their photograph taken, do not ignore this. The islanders are warm and hospitable and if you stop and spend some time finding out what they are doing, they will usually then allow a photograph.

POLICE

Police Headquarters is in Upper Bay Street, Kingstown ☎ 457-1211.

PORTS

The main port is Kingstown although there are yacht facilities and jetties around St Vincent and throughout the Grenadines. There is a marina in Bequia with repair facilities.

POST OFFICES

Post Office hours are 8.30am to 3pm Monday to Friday and Saturday 8.30am to 11.30am. The General Post Office is in Halifax Street in Kingstown, and there are sub-post offices in all towns and villages.

PUBLIC HOLIDAYS & FESTIVALS

(Check locally to confirm times and dates.)

January
January 1 New Year's Day
Janaury 22 St Vincent and the
             Grenadines Day

March
National Music Festival

April
Good Friday
Easter Monday
Easter Regatta — Bequia

May
May 1   Labour Day

June
Whit Monday

July
Carnival
CARICOM DAY

August
August Bank Holiday
Canouan Regatta

September
National Dance Festival

October
National Drama Festival
27 October   Independence Day

December
Decemebr 25 Christmas Day
December 26 Boxing Day
December 31 New Year's Eve
              Celebrations

PUBLIC TOILETS

There are not many public toilets on the islands, but bars, restaurants and hotels have private facilities which can usually be used if you ask politely.

RESTAURANTS

There is a remarkably large choice when it comes to eating out on the island. There are the inevitable fast food burger, pizza and fried chicken outlets, beach cafes offering excellent value for the money and elegant upmarket dining rooms, as well as restaurants offering a wide range of ethnic cuisines, from creole and Caribbean cooking to Chinese. Most accept credit cards and during peak times of the year, reservations are recommended. If you come across a restaurant not listed in the guide, or have comments about any of those that are, I would very much like to hear from you.

The restaurants listed in the itineraries are classified by price

$ = inexpensive
$$ = moderate
$$$ = expensive.

SECURITY

St Vincent has a low crime rate but it makes sense, like anywhere else, not to walk around wearing expensive jewellery or flashing large sums of money.

Do not carry around your passport, travellers cheques or all your money. Keep them secure in your room or in a hotel safety deposit box. It is also a good idea to have photocopies of the information page of your passport, your air ticket and holiday insurance policy. All will help greatly if the originals are lost.

As with most tourist destinations, you might be pestered by touts trying to sell tours, souvenirs and even drugs, or by young people begging. A firm 'no' or 'not interested', is normally enough to persuade them to try someone else.

Do not be alarmed at the large number of people who walk around with machetes. These are widely used as gardening implements.

SERVICE CHARGES & TAXES

There is a Government tax of 7 per cent on hotel and restaurant bills, and a service charge of 10 per cent is usually added. Menus and tariffs sometimes include these charges, so check to make sure they have not been added again. In shops, the price on the label is what you pay. When buying in markets and from street vendors, try haggling over the price.

SIGHTSEEING

Sightseeing and island tours by land or sea can be organised through hotels, tour representatives or one of the many specialist tour companies on the island (see Tour Operators).

Many companies also offer boat trips to explore secluded beaches not accessible by road, and other islands. These include:

Anchorage Yacht Club
Union Island
☎ 458-8221

Baleine Tours
☎ 457-4089

Dive St Vincent
☎ 457-4714

Dennis' Hideaway
☎ 458-8594

Grand View Beach Hotel
☎ 458-4811

Grenadines Dive
Union Island
☎ 458-8138

Sea Breeze
☎ 458-4969

Dive Canouan
☎ 458-8648

SPORT

Cricket is the national game and played with such fervour that it is not surprising that the West Indies are world champions. The game is played at every opportunity and anywhere. You can be driving in the countryside and find players using the road as a pitch. It is played on the beach — even in the water if the tide is coming in. If the island team or the West Indies is playing, almost all the radios on the island are tuned in for the commentary. When cricket is not being played, football is the top sport. Also popular are volleyball, basketball and netball.

For the visitor, there is a huge range of sporting opportunities from swimming and scuba diving, to horseback riding and hiking, to golf and tennis. There is cycling, sailing, squash and, of course, fishing either from shore or boat. The Atlantic coastline offers stronger swell for windsurfing and surfing but the seas can sometimes be very rough and care is needed, while the Caribbean beaches offer safe swimming. Swimming in slow moving rivers and lakes is not advisable because of the risk of bilharzia, a disease caused by a parasitic water-borne worm.

Most hotels offer a variety of sports and water activities, and there are diving schools where you can learn what it is all about and progress to advanced level if you have the time.

Cycling
Cycling is a good way to get around especially on the Grenadines where there is much less motor traffic. On St Vincent

care needs to be exercised when cycling on busy roads. Bikes can be hired from the Sailors Cycle Centre on St Vincent, ☎ 457-1712, and from the Lighthouse on Bequia, ☎ 458-3084.

Fitness Gyms/Exercise Centres

Grand View Hotel Health Club and Sauna
Villa Point, St Vincent

Hiking

Walking is great fun and there are lots of official trails, especially in the mountains. Some hikes rquire a great deal of physical fitness so check first. It is also advisable to use the services of a guide on some of the longer interior hikes. Guides are not expensive, are very knowledgeable and work hard to ensure you get the most out of your trip. When walking inland, it is a good idea to wear long trousers and carry a waterproof top and light jumper. Stout footwear is essential. Wear a hat if not used to being out in the sun, use sun screen and insect repellant. Make sure you have adequate drinking supplies, if water is not available along the way.

Horseback Riding

Cotton House Hotel
Mustique

Scuba Diving

Diving Centres include:

Bequia Dive Resort
Friendship Bay, Bequia
☎ 458-3249

Dive Anchorage
Anchorage Yacht Club
Union Island
☎ 458-8221

Dive St Vincent
Young Island Dock, St Vincent
☎ 457-4714

Dive Bequia
Belmont, Bequia
☎ 458-3504

Dive Canouan
Canouan
☎ 458-8648

Dive Paradise
Bequia
☎ 458-3563

Grenadine Dives
Union Island
☎ 458-8138

Petit Byahaut
St Vincent
☎ 458-7008

St Vincent Dive Experience
Blue Lagoon, St Vincent
☎ 456-9741

Sunsports
Port Elizabeth, Bequia
☎ 458-3577

Cricket is played wherever there is a flat space

Squash

Cecil Cyrus Squash Complex
Grand View Beach Hotel
St Vincent

Prospect Racquet Club
St Vincent

Tennis

Many resorts and large hotels have their own tennis courts, often floodlit.

St Vincent
Grand View Beach Hotel
Kingstown Tennis Club
Prospect Racquet Club
Young Island Resort

Bequia
Friendship Bay Hotel
Plantation House
Spring on Bequia
Sunsports

Canouan
Canouan Beach Club

Mustique
Cotton House Hotel

Palm Island
Palm Island Beach Club

Petit St Vincent
Petit St Vincent Resort

Watersports

Available at all resorts and most large hotels, and through most tour and dive operators.

TELEPHONES

If you wondered where Britain's red telephone boxes went, the answer is that many ended up in St Vincent. There are lots of public telephones on the island, operated by Cable and Wireless and most accept coins and phone cards. Phone cards can be purchased at hotels, shops, airports, marinas and tourist offices. The phone cards can also be used on most of the English-speaking Windward Islands.

Faxes can be sent from most hotels and faxes, telexes and computer data transmission services are available from the Cable & Wireless office in Halifax Street, Kingstown. If you have any communications problems, visit their offices where you will find them most helpful.

The international dialling code for St Vincent is 1 809. From the United States, dialling to St Vincent is a long distance call, dial 1 809 and the seven digit number. From the United Kingdom 001 1 809 and then the number. To use AT&T USA Direct Service, dial 1-800-872-2881 from public phones only and then follow the recorded instructions. International calls are charged by the full minute, and a 10 per cent Government tax is added.

TIME

St Vincent is in the Atlantic Standard Time Zone which is four hours behind Greenwich Mean Time and one hour ahead of Eastern Time in the United States. If it is noon in London then it is 8am in St. Vincent, and when it is noon in New York, it is 1pm on the island.

While it is important to know the time so that you do not miss your flight, time becomes less important the longer you stay on the islands. If you order a taxi it will generally be early or arrive on time, and if you have a business meeting it will start on schedule. For almost everything else be prepared to adopt 'Caribbean time', especially in bars, restaurants and shops. Do not confuse this relaxed attitude with laziness or rudeness, it is just the way things are done in the islands, and the quicker you accept this, the sooner you will start to relax and enjoy yourselves.

TIPPING

Tips are not generally added to bills but it is customary to tip bell hops in hotels, taxi drivers, guides and other people providing a service. Tip taxi drivers around 10 per cent, bell hops EC$1-2 for each piece of luggage, and if there is no service charge added to your restaurant bill, leave 10-15per cent depending on how much you enjoyed the meal.

TOURIST INFORMATION OFFICES

Tourist Offices in the West Indies

St Vincent
Bay Street, Kingstown
☎ 457-1502
Open Monday to Friday 8am to noon and 1pm to 4.15pm.

E. T. Joshua Airport
☎ 458-4685

Bequia
Tourist Bureau, Port Elizabeth
☎ 458-3286
Open Sunday to Friday 9am to 12.30pm and 1.30pm to 4pm. Saturday 9am to 12.30pm.

Union Island
Tourist Bureau
☎ 458-8350
Open daily 8am-noon, 1pm-4pm.

Barbados
Grantley Adams International Airport
Arrivals hall
☎ 428-0961
Open daily 1pm until the last flight to St Vincent has boarded.

Tourist Offices Abroad

United Kingdom
10 Kensington Court
London, W8 5DL
☎ 0171-937-6570

United States of America
801 Second Avenue
21st Floor, New York, NY 10017
☎ 1-800-729-1726

6505 Cove Creek Place
Dallas, Texas, TX 75240
☎ 214-239-6451

Canada
32 Park Road
Toronto, Ontario M4W 2N4
☎ 416-924-5796

Germany
Wurmbergstrasse 26
D-7032 Sindelfingen
☎ 70-3180-6260

TOUR OPERATORS

There are many tour operators on the island and all offer a number of trips and excursions, or can make itineraries to suit individual requirements. Many of the tours sound the same, so check to see that you are getting value for money, or getting something special. Main operators are:

St Vincent

W. J. Abbott
Upper Bay Street, Kingstown
☎ 456-1511

Baleine Tours
Villa Beach
☎ 457-4089

Barefoot Holidays
Blue Lagoon
☎ 456-9334

Caribbean International Travel Services
Granby Street, Kingstown
☎ 457-1841

Corea & Co
Halifax Street, Kingstown
☎ 456-1201

Emerald Travel & Tours
Halifax Street, Kingstown
☎ 457-1996

Global Travel Service
White Chapel, Kingstown
☎ 456-1601

Grenadines Travel Co
Amos Vale
☎ 458-4818

Kim's Rental
Grenville Street, Kingstown
☎ 456-1884

Paradise Tours
PO Box 280
Kingstown
☎ 458-5545

Travel World
Bay Street, Kingstown
☎ 456-2600

Universal Travel
Bay Street, Kingstown
☎ 457-2779

Bequia

Grenadines Travel
Port Elizabeth
☎ 458-3795

Union Island

Eagles Travel
Clifton
☎ 458-8179

WEDDINGS

St Vincent and the Grenadines are a popular destination for honeymoon couples, and lots of other couples get carried away by the romance of the island and decide to marry while on vacation. If you decide to marry, you must file an application to be married after you have been resident on the island for at least three days. This application for either a church or civil wedding, must be made with the appropriate fee to the Ministry of Justice and a special Governor General's licence is required. The licence is then valid for three months. Some hotels will help with weddings and make all the arrangements for you.

Most denominations of church weddings can be arranged in advance, and registrars usually charge a fee plus travel costs. Valentine's Day is a very popular day for weddings, and registrars are usually very busy rushing around conducting marriage after marriage. The Registry is open Monday to Friday 9am to noon and 1pm to 3pm, and on Saturday 9am to 11am.

YACHT CHARTER & PRIVATE MOORINGS

There is a huge range of vessels and crews for charter for sailing, sightseeing, fishing and diving. Marigot Bay and Rodney Bay, both on the north-western coast, are the two most popular marinas.

Companies offering yacht charters are:

Barefoot Yacht Charters
Blue Lagoon, St Vincent
☎ 456-9526

Lagoon Marina and Hotel
St Vincent
☎ 458-4308
Both the above companies offer bareboat and crewed charters.

Frangipani Yacht Services
Bequia
☎ 458-3244

Anchorage Yacht Club
Union Island
☎ 458-8221

Index

A
Argyle Beach 76

B
Baleine Falls 69

Balliceaux 100
Barrouallie 68-69
Battowia 100
Bequia 10, 87-96, 90, 95
 Admiralty Bay 92

Anchorage Bay 92
Friendship Bay 92
Hope Bay 92
Lower Bay 92
Mount Pleasant 93

Port Elizabeth 92, 93
Princess Margaret
  Beach 92
Spring Bay 93
Biabou 76
Black Point 77
Blue Lagoon 73
Buccament 65
Byera Bay 77

C

Cable Hut Bay 73
Calliaqua 73
Calliaqua Bay 72
Campden Park 53
Canouan 96-97
Chateaubelair 69, 78
Colonarie 77
Commantawana Bay
  81

D

Dorsetshire Hill 72

F

Fancy 81
Fort Duvernette 10, 72-73

G

Georgetown 77, 78
Grand Sable 77
Grant's Bay 76
Grenadines 87-105

K

Kingstown 52-57
  Anglican Cathedral
    56
  Archaeological
    Museum 61
  Botanical Gardens
    10, 58-59, 60-61
  Court House 56
  Fort Charlotte 57-60
  Grenadines Wharf
    53
  Little Tokyo 56
  Market 56
  Methodist Church
    56
  Roman Catholic
    Cathedral 57
  St Vincent Crafts-
    men's Centre 64
  Victoria Park 57

L

Layou 10, 65-68

M

Marriaqua Valley. See
  Mesopotamia
Mayreau 100
Mesopotamia 73-76
Montreal 76
Mustique 97-100
  Britannia Bay 97
  Endeavour Bay 97
  Lagoon Bay 97
  Lovell Village 99
  Plantation Bay 97

N

North Union 76

P

Palm Island 101

Peruvian Vale 76
Petit Byahaut 64
Petit St Vincent 101-102
Prune Island. See Palm
  Island

R

Rabacca Dry River 78
Ribisti 73
Richmond 69
Richmond Vale 78

S

Sandy Bay 80
Sans 76
Sharp's Bay 73
Souci 76
Soufriere 10, 78, 78-80
South Union 76
St Vincent 47-85

T

Tobago Cays 101
Trinity Falls 69

U

Union Island 102-105
  Clifton 104

V

Vermont 10, 65
Villa 72

W

Wallilabou Bay 69

Y

Yambou Gorge 76
Young Island 10, 72

Caribbean Sunseeker

For sun and fun on your island destination, let our *Caribbean Sunseeker* series be your guide. These books have been carefully researched to bring you the best and most accurate information available. This series will include at least the following titles. Check with your bookseller for availability of new titles.

Antigua & Barbuda

Bahamas

Barbados

Bermuda

Cayman Islands

Cuba

Dominica

Dominican Republic

Dutch Antilles

Florida Keys

Grenada

Jamaica

Puerto Rico

St Lucia

St Vincent & the Grenadines

Tobago

Trinidad

US Virgin Islands